IT'S YOUR WEALTH

KEEP IT

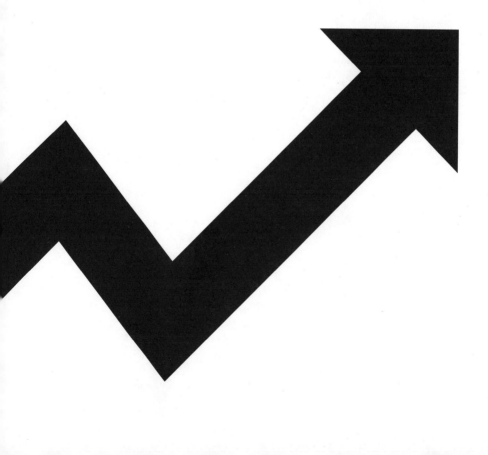

IT'S YOUR WEALTH

KEEP IT

THE DEFINITIVE GUIDE
TO GROWING, PROTECTING,
ENJOYING, AND PASSING ON
YOUR WEALTH

JOHN L. SMALLWOOD, CFP®

Advantage.

Published by Advantage, Charleston, South Carolina.
Member of Advantage Media Group.

ADVANTAGE is a registered trademark, and the Advantage colophon is a trademark of Advantage Media Group, Inc.

Printed in the United States of America.

10 9 8 7 6 5 4 3 2

ISBN: 978-1-64225-098-5
LCCN: 2020902978

Cover and layout design by David Taylor.

This publication is designed to provide accurate and authoritative information in regard to the subject matter covered. It is sold with the understanding that the publisher is not engaged in rendering legal, accounting, or other professional services. If legal advice or other expert assistance is required, the services of a competent professional person should be sought.

Advantage Media Group is proud to be a part of the Tree Neutral® program. Tree Neutral offsets the number of trees consumed in the production and printing of this book by taking proactive steps such as planting trees in direct proportion to the number of trees used to print books. To learn more about Tree Neutral, please visit **www.treeneutral.com**.

Advantage Media Group is a publisher of business, self-improvement, and professional development books and online learning. We help entrepreneurs, business leaders, and professionals share their Stories, Passion, and Knowledge to help others Learn & Grow. Do you have a manuscript or book idea that you would like us to consider for publishing? Please visit **advantagefamily.com** or call **1.866.775.1696**.

CONTENTS

INTRODUCTION

HAMMERS AND ARTISTS

There are two times in a man's life when he should not speculate: when he can't afford it, and when he can.

—Mark Twain

My father used to say, "Give me the best tools and the best wood, and I could build a crude table that will be uneven and lopsided and downright ugly. Give the same tools and the same wood to a fine craftsman, you might get a Louis XV armoire."

The point was that creating a real work of art is not just about the knowledge and tools a person has; it's about understanding how to organize and plan details, and then seeing a project through to its completion.

My father was a wealth manager himself, so I basically lived and breathed wealth management from an early age. That gave me a deeper understanding and more confidence than most people in

1

wealth management. It made me more than a craftsman at a trade. I have an interest, devotion, and level of experience that make me a true *artist* as a wealth manager.

My father also taught me the meaning of success—and failure. He believed that in order to succeed—and to appreciate your successes—you have to make mistakes. In fact, he wanted me to fail and learn from the failure. He thought that a little bit of pain along the way would make the successes greater and longer lasting.

What I came to understand was that financial planning is about relationships, about getting to know people and their circumstances. It's not just a transaction business. It's not just about selling an insurance policy or investment and then moving on. It's about building a lifetime plan—together. That was the definition of success instilled in me early by my father, who often said, "We don't care about selling very quickly today. What we care about is doing the right thing for the client today so that they'll come back tomorrow. They'll be a client for life, and they'll refer you to other people. That's how you build a successful practice." Putting the client first: that's what he defined as success.

Today, I have clients that I've been advising for more than twenty-nine years, including many who were my father's clients.

YOUR BACKCOUNTRY GUIDE

As a wealth manager, my job is to be your backcountry guide in helping you grow, protect, and keep your wealth. I'm going to help keep you from sliding down into a crevasse. I'm here to be the sounding board about your financial situation, to help you talk through your circumstances, build a plan, and keep that plan current and ever evolving—just like your life.

That outlook on financial planning and wealth management started very early. I began working with my father in 1989 during the summer break from college. Back then, I would go out and talk to employees of companies about payroll deduction options for disability insurance and life insurance. We spoke to hundreds of employees about their ability to earn income being their most important asset, using the "One-Hundred-Man Story" to make a point. The story goes as follows: Out of one hundred working people at retirement age, one is wealthy, four are financially secure, five keep working because they have to (not because they want to), thirty-six are deceased, and more than half—fifty-four—are broke. That last group depends on Social Security, friends and relatives, and charities just to stay afloat. After working for forty years, most people don't have enough money saved to live a good retirement. Only 5 percent have enough to maintain their standard of living. Less than 1 percent of people accumulate real wealth.[1] The story has not changed. The Social Security Administration recently updated the study, and the results are as dismal, despite more information, cheaper fees on investments, and other factors. It's a real problem. We need to change behaviors so that we can change the outcome for participants.

The story about the average working person's wealth really began to help me see that people in the workforce were woefully underprepared for what was coming and really not aware of how much money they would need for all the future aims they want to achieve—college, weddings, retirement, just life in general.

I committed full time to the financial services industry in 1990 when I graduated from Bentley College. There were many different

---

1   "Income of the Population 55 or Older, 2012," SSA Publication no. 13-11871, April 2014.

routes I could have taken at the time, but in studying them all, I found that most people in the industry offered one product. They basically had a hammer that they sold to everyone. Whether it was an annuity, life insurance, mutual fund, or some other kind of superstar investment, one hammer was badged and rebadged as some sort of magic or miracle product that would save a person's retirement. Just put all your money in this hammer, and you'll be fine. So not true!

Yes, all those products can help you, but on their own, they don't address your unique circumstances, your unique dynamics, and the way your plan is laid out. Your kids, your spouse, your parents, your siblings—all of these impact your circumstances and how your money is organized. That's what dictates the success of your plan.

My father had a macro view of wealth management. Early in my career, when I was twenty-two, he sent me to Atlantic City to attend a three-day event being put on by Robert Castiglione. Castiglione created a unique financial model called the Protection Savings and Growth Model. I was introduced to him, and in our first conversation, he told me, "You are young; people will not believe you, but stay strong in your conviction, and time will be on your side." His thinking was unlike anything in the industry: he blended economics with financial strategies. He became a mentor to me, and his training helped solidify what my father and I were doing.

Everything in your plan is impacted by decisions you make. Most financial plans focus on a very narrow set of variables, but that kind of thinking can set a plan up for failure. True success comes from looking at the variables and the impact that changing one or more variables can have on a plan.

My father was focused on the client reaching full financial potential by blending products together in a unique way that is customized to each client. He and I started looking at how all the financial products could come together in a unique way to reach seven goals:

1. Reduce taxes.

2. Reduce risk.

3. Reduce fees and costs.

4. Increase your savings rate.

5. Increase your retirement income.

6. Put more benefits and protection around your wealth.

7. Pass more money on to the family.

What we found is most financial strategies do the exact opposite of these things. A macro view of wealth management, on the other hand, maximizes the efficiency of every dollar. A plan that has a macro view does the following:

- Gets the best tax benefits by taking advantage of all tax deductions.

- Limits risk and reduces volatility by diversifying asset-class investing, spreading out money over different types of stocks: large cap, small cap, mid cap, value, growth, international, and emerging markets.

- Reduces fees and costs by identifying and eliminating or reducing the impact of leaks in the plan.

- Allows for a savings rate of 15 percent or more, growing as income grows. If you make $100,000 annually, you should be saving $15,000 per year. If you make more, your savings rate should increase, getting close to 30 percent as you move above $750,000 annual income.

- Has 50 percent or more of annual income in liquid savings to allow access to funds immediately, funds that are free of market volatility.

- Maximizes retirement income through strategies such as having 25 percent of invested assets in whole life insurance with cash value and a permanent death benefit for life.

- Puts more protection around your wealth. That includes maximizing insurance coverage at the lowest cost possible—property and casualty coverage, umbrella liability, disability and long-term care, and life insurance coverage during all phases of life. It also employs wills and trusts.

- Maximizes participation in company retirement plans, taking advantage of any match.

- Takes advantage of market changes over the course of the plan by undergoing an annual review.

A BETTER WAY

The difference between financial planning and wealth management is in the titles: finances versus wealth. Managing finances deals with the goal of trying to get ahead. Managing wealth is all about building a legacy. Wealth management at its core is about you. It involves a philosophy that encompasses not only your cash flows, but involves your beliefs, interests, and goals.

As a Certified Financial Planner (CFP®), I have a fiduciary responsibility to provide my clients with the best financial advice. But I do that with a grand-scheme view of wealth management. That doesn't mean offering the same hammer as a magic tool to solve every client's problems.

It pisses me off when I see a CFP with only one product to sell—and new clients come in with one product in their portfolio. They've bought life insurance or company stock, and then a fiduciary has convinced them to get out of that product and buy theirs because it's the easiest way to make a sale. I can hear the conversation now: "Hey, you're spending $20,000 a year on a life insurance policy, and you've got $300,000 in cash. We can take that $300,000, put it in a different policy or another investment product, and now you can spend $5,000 a year." They're not adding on; they're taking away— and the client ends up losing because of it. Instead, the fiduciary should be looking at the product itself, whereby the conversation might then go, "Hey, that's a really good product. But I think you need additional coverage, and let me tell you why."

I have a full complement of licenses that allows me to offer products that are appropriate for each individual client. Through my registered investment advisory firm, my team and I do financial planning and wealth management that is about who you are, what your finances are made up of, and what products, investments, and strategies can come together to provide you with a plan that will meet those seven fundamental goals: reduce taxes, reduce risk, reduce fees and costs while increasing your savings rate, increase your retirement income, put more benefits and protection around your wealth, and ultimately pass more to your family.

With all there is to consider about a person's situation, the industry still focuses on single-product sales and making rate of return the end-all-be-all. But as I write this book, there are a couple of big crises looming.

One involves a whole series of private pensions through large corporations such as GE. At one point, GE had an $11 billion surplus in its retirement plan. Today, it has more than six hundred thousand active retirees and another eighty-five thousand employees who are counting on that pension when they retire. The problem? The plan has a $32 billion deficit. That's just one company. There are a number of private, state-level, and multi-employer pensions with deficits—and they had some of the best investment management. If these pension funds couldn't make the numbers work, what hope does the average person have?

The other crisis is that retirement is going to cost a lot more money than most people realize. It's almost impossible to imagine getting to a magic age of sixty or seventy, quitting work, and living out retirement in comfort. That's like the plans that were being put together when I started in this industry.

Back then, most plans were designed to run out of money by age eighty-five. But people are living a lot longer today. Living to one hundred is not out of the question.

Here are a couple of plans to show you how some restructuring can make all the difference in how well your plan performs.

Plan A: Using a $1 million target, and focusing primarily on a 3.5 percent rate of return per year, there is a better than 70 percent chance of running out of money in the first twenty-five years of retirement. I frequently encounter people who spend thirty-five or forty years working for XYZ, and they've accumulated a $500,000 house, about $50,000 in cash at the bank, and a 401(k) plan with 90 percent of assets allocated to the stock market. There's no protection in that strategy, and the only inflation hedge is hope.

Plan B: By structuring a plan to have the same $500,000 house, a $100,000 retirement safety buffer, and $250,000 in whole life insurance cash values with a death benefit of $900,000 paid up, you've got $250,000 sitting in guaranteed income products, and the remainder of the $450,000 remains in the same asset allocation strategy. There are many things we can do with the life insurance death benefit that can help offset the long-term care costs—that can be a permission slip to take on a reverse mortgage, to do a charitable remainder trust, to do all kinds of advanced planning strategies. Now you can take your 3 to 4 percent withdrawal with the $250,000 guaranteed income and never run out of capital. With everything side by side, you can have substantially higher enjoyment and still have inflation hedges, backup, and protection, and you can pass more on to the family.

The bottom line is that you need structure to protect yourself from earthquakes—a rocky stock market, hyperinflation, war, sideways markets—all the things that are so dangerous to a retirement plan. In my examples, Plan A has no protection; it's going to get decimated. Plan B has foundation, structure, redundancies, protections, and things that make it so bulletproof to the financial pressures that are out there.

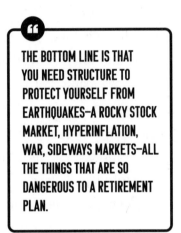

> **THE BOTTOM LINE IS THAT YOU NEED STRUCTURE TO PROTECT YOURSELF FROM EARTHQUAKES—A ROCKY STOCK MARKET, HYPERINFLATION, WAR, SIDEWAYS MARKETS—ALL THE THINGS THAT ARE SO DANGEROUS TO A RETIREMENT PLAN.**

People are often led into a false sense of safety that one magic investment is going to save their life. At my firm, we don't think that there is only one way to get things done; we think there are many ways to get it done. There are a lot of really good financial strategies out there, and when they are all put together, they're even better. Layer two, three, four, five, six financial strategies together, and bring together multiple financial products designed to do all those benefits. Now, you've got a plan. An amazing plan. By applying macroeconomics, as Castiglione taught me, one dollar can work like three or four dollars in your plan.

That's the difference between having a micro and macro view. And it's the difference between financial planning and wealth management.

Clients often bring in spreadsheets containing their financial plan. God love them, they're great spreadsheets. They're some of the most beautiful spreadsheets that I've ever seen in my entire life. The only problem is that they are linear. They've got a flat rate of return of 6 percent, a flat tax rate (or no taxes), a static inflation rate. If I take that plan and realistically modify one of those elements, then the whole plan is thrown off.

People don't really think through what they're doing. They don't think through their strategies. They don't understand the impact of inflation. They don't understand the impact of market volatility or sideways markets. They don't understand how financially devastating a long-term disability could be. They don't understand how long-term care is going to affect them.

The problem is that they are basing their future wealth on a simple formula:

Money × *Time* × *Percent of Return* = *Future Wealth*

This formula states that your financial plan consists of investing money with a projected return. Using this formula, you should end up with amount X of future wealth, which is not how reality works. What happens if your rate of return changes for the worse? What if the time to meet the projected financial goal is cut short? What if the amount of money you have changes? Changing one variable changes the outcome; changing two variables destroys your plan.

> CHECK OUT MY WEBSITE FOR AN ANIMATED VIDEO ILLUSTRATING THE WEALTH CURVE CONCEPTS: SMALLWOODASSOCIATES.COM.

The key is to understand all the variables and develop strategies to mitigate and offset or reduce the impact of all these different things that are going to happen that can't be predicted. Yet there is no telling what is going to happen at the end of the day. The markets are down as I write these words. Where will they be a month from now? A year from now? When you retire?

YOUR FINANCIAL WORK OF ART

As human beings, when it comes to retirement, we always think it's a trade-off—if I want more retirement income, I have to leave less to my family. If I want to leave more to my family, that means less retirement income for me. If I want to hit my goals, I've got to take on more risk. But those assumptions are not necessarily true. It really depends on the individual.

Everyone is different. Every financial plan should also be different. Creating a financial work of art means peeling back the layers on your financial life and looking at current and past circumstances, then chiseling away what's not great about a plan. *A financial plan is a work of art because the unique dynamics of the individual dictate the outcome of that plan.*

Early on in my career, Dan Sullivan of the Strategic Coach® exposed me to the concept of Unique Ability® and surrounding yourself with a unique team. His concepts of The Gap™; vision, opposition, transformation, and action (VOTA®); and Strategy Circle® are extremely valuable in thinking and growing business and wealth. The goal is to free you up so you can focus on your highest and best use and where you get the most enjoyment. As a business owner or high-level corporate executive, you need to focus on growing your business and making it more profitable. Having a wealth plan that you are confident in frees you to do just that.

With every client, we dig into any existing plan to create a balance today, tomorrow, and every year to come. We want to work together to build and execute a plan, and then constantly refine it based on your life changes. That plan must have multiple financial products coming together to help reduce taxes, reduce risk, reduce fees and costs, while increasing your savings rate and retirement income, putting more benefits and protection around your wealth, and ultimately passing more to your family. That's really the ultimate goal. If you're not trying to get to that point, then at least save yourself some time right now. Stop reading, throw this book in the fireplace, and move on.

FOR A NO-COST, NO-OBLIGATION CONSULT WITH A SMALLWOOD WEALTH MANAGEMENT FINANCIAL ADVISOR, CALL 1-800-797-1000.

But if you want a big-picture approach to wealth management, if you want to understand all the aspects of your financial circumstances and have a plan that truly speaks to you about your life, then read on.

CHAPTER ONE

THE WEALTH CURVE–A VISUAL OF YOUR FINANCIAL LIFE

You should expect your retirement to last longer than you originally thought it would, cost more than you imagined and planned for, and require different financial strategies than anybody else is talking to you about.

Everyone has a Wealth Curve—it's a visual that is created based on our financial life and the pressures that impact our wealth and its potential.

That Wealth Curve starts when we enter the working world and get our first paycheck. Suddenly, we become aware of money. Every decision we make from that point on impacts our wealth. We start putting money away and hope for a high rate of return on our investments—that's how we'll accumulate the wealth we need to one day leave the rat race, enjoy retirement, and still leave a legacy to our family.

One of the fundamentals to understanding how to grow wealth is that you are the single most important part of your financial plan. Your ability to earn income and save money impacts your entire world. That income may come from being a business owner working hard to keep the doors open, or from being an employee working for someone else.

Then, life happens. Before we know it, your wealth isn't growing as expected. It's not a steady curve trending upward. Without really understanding what's going on, there is a tremendous and unexplainable amount of financial pressure pushing down on your Wealth Curve and its potential. That's the second fundamental to understand about growing wealth—factors are applying pressure to your finances, preventing your Wealth Curve from growing exponentially. Taxes, fees, interest on credit cards, hidden expenses, mortgages, car loans, student loans, insurance premiums, market volatility, loss of employment, underemployment, inflation, technological changes, cell phones and data plans. Over time, everything we own wears out and needs to be replaced—at a much higher cost, thanks to inflation. The pressure is coming from more than just our own lives; often we're paying for others—college for the kids, weddings and sweet sixteens, parents or other family members who need help. Not to mention the impact of long-term care, disability, lawsuits, and estate taxes.

All of this pressure mounts as our income and wealth grow. Predicting the sequences in which things happen and their outcomes is impossible. For many people the pressure becomes so great that their curve collapses. Their wealth begins to deteriorate, and they run out of assets.

Because of the unique web of who you are, the components of your financial plan are different from those of your parents, your siblings, your neighbors, your friends. And because you are unique, your financial plan has different financial pressures placed on it. All of those affect your curve.

To be successful, we have to factor all of these pressures into a financial plan. *Your output is the product of all of your decisions.* In that sense, *you are the product.* Your success doesn't come from one decision that you make, but it's numerous decisions that you make every single day over your entire financial life. That starts the moment you walk out the door of your parents' house and take full responsibility for yourself—and your family. That's your financial life.

Now that you know about the Wealth Curve—what direction is yours trending?

FINANCIAL PLANNING—NO "MAGIC" SOLUTIONS

Too often, people are siloed in their view of their financial plan rather than focused on the big picture. Sometimes, it's because they believe in a pitch that one magic product or investment is going to save their retirement. Whether it's a mutual fund, insurance policy, annuity, stock option, 401(k), or something else, the truth is that banking entirely on a single product or type of investment is setting you up for financial failure.

There is no magic wand that you can wave and save your financial plan. The "magic" that is going to save your retirement is to put multiple products and multiple strategies together in an integrated way that is unique to you, the individual.

Fortunately, I recognized that early in my career.

I was working with an attorney on their client's estate plan. The client was worth about $10 million at the time and had a lot of illiquid assets, most of which was in their business. The business was really centered on the client, and he needed to buy life insurance. At the time, about $1.3 million could be exempted from inheritance tax.

> **THERE IS NO MAGIC WAND THAT YOU CAN WAVE AND SAVE YOUR FINANCIAL PLAN. THE "MAGIC" THAT IS GOING TO SAVE YOUR RETIREMENT IS TO PUT MULTIPLE PRODUCTS AND MULTIPLE STRATEGIES TOGETHER IN AN INTEGRATED WAY THAT IS UNIQUE TO YOU, THE INDIVIDUAL.**

The attorney came to me and said that they wanted the client to buy a second-to-die life insurance policy. That was the hot product at the time. It was very popular way to take care of inheritance tax. The policy would insure both husband and wife and would pay when the second spouse died.

But I kept telling them that it was not really an appropriate financial strategy. The husband had some savings, and together they had a decent lifestyle. However, the main asset in the client's life— the business—was illiquid. If he died prior to the business being sold, it would probably die with him because he was the major driver.

Instead of a second-to-die policy, I told everyone in the room that the policy should be a "first to die." What the client really needed was money on the first death. If the husband, the business owner, died first, the spouse would need the money on his death because the business would struggle.

As with any insurance policy, it required paying premiums. The client needed $3 million worth of insurance, which meant a second-to-die premium was around $30,000. For the same $3 million, the first-to-die policy premium was around $60,000.

When I explained that the first-to-die policy was a better option, all of a sudden the situation degraded into a huge argument. "You just want to sell a bigger premium," the attorneys shouted at me. I was twentysomething at the time, and they were trying to bully me into doing what they thought was best, not what I knew was best. "Just do the second-to-die policy and shut up. What do you know?" one of the attorneys said to me.

"No, I'm not doing it, because it's not right," I said. "If you die, sir," I told the client, "your wife's going to get a bill for the $30,000 premium, and she's not going to have any liquidity because everything is tied up in your business. And since we can't guarantee that it will sell for a reasonable price, she's going to be left with a big problem."

At that point, the attorneys told me to write the policy or get out. "All right, I'm out of here," I said.

As I was packing up my papers and getting ready to leave, the client spoke up. "Wait a minute," he said. "You're going to walk away from a commission?"

"Yes," I told him. "Because it's not right."

The client saw the value in what I was saying because after I left, he fired the attorneys and got new attorneys, and I ended up writing a first-to-die policy for him. Many years later, that policy actually paid off. As it turned out, he had some other issues along the way, and the state tax laws changed, so in the end, it all worked out even better than originally planned.

The moral of the story? There are always very popular products being pushed—everyone wants to treat clients with cookie-cutter solutions. But every client isn't the same—everyone has a different lifestyle, different circumstances, and different financial pressures. A single solution isn't right for everyone. Single products are often focused very tightly on rate of return. But they don't look at everything that's happening in a person's life. They don't look at the financial pressures or erosion principles—those are actually taking away more wealth than is being accumulated in most cases.

Car insurance is a simple example of something that often takes away more wealth than is being accumulated. If a forty-year-old individual has an annual premium of $800 and drives for forty years, that's $32,000 on premiums. If a catastrophe happens—a huge tree limb falls in an ice storm and crushes the car—then paying $32,000 over forty years makes sense. But if nothing ever happens, that's $32,000 spent with nothing in return—basically buying a car that is never driven. Plus, there's no opportunity to put that money in something that will bring any sort of gain.

If that money were put into an investment that had an 8 percent return over that same forty years, you'd have a gain of $207,000. That's a lost opportunity, because that gain has been transferred to the insurance company.

You don't want to go without car insurance—you don't want that exposure. But maybe you can reduce your premiums from $800 to $700, a simple move that, over the years, can save almost $27,000.

This is just one example of how capital erodes. Financial institutions have fees and other costs that are designed to transfer the wealth from you to them. The government's taking your money in the form of taxes: income tax, sales taxes, consumption taxes.

Many of us feel the crunch from all this pressure, but we don't do anything about it. It's like the biology experiment with a pot of water and a frog. Boil the water first, and then try throwing in the frog. He'll struggle to keep you from tossing him in and will jump out if you do. But if you put the frog in lukewarm water and then start turning up the heat, the frog will get so accustomed to the water temperature that as it heats up, he will slowly boil to death.

That's what happens with so many people and their financial plans. They get so comfortable with their situation, even though erosion keeps heating up the water, that they end up at the boiling point—they've got no money left.

Life gets busy—I get it. But all the while, your wealth is being systematically transferred away and eroding your future.

YOUR WEALTH UNDER ATTACK

As humans, we are trained to always look at life from a positive perspective. When it comes to investing, we're always geared toward looking at a glossy past performance. But that's only giving one side of the story. A mutual fund might have had an average rate of return over the past twenty years of 12 percent, so you might want to put money in it and expect that it will give a 12 percent rate of return and you'll retire comfortably. But that equation is missing many variables.

Once pressures are applied to an investment—those pressures I mentioned at the beginning of the chapter—then the outcome can be completely different than what you were expecting.

For example, a $400,000 portfolio for an investor might have nearly a 12 percent rate of return over a twenty-five-year period from 1994 to 2017, compounding it to more than $5.3 million. That "simple math" looks really good on a spreadsheet. But the truth is, that nearly 12 percent rate of return didn't happen every year. In 2002, for instance, the market was down 22.1 percent at the end of the year. It rebounded the following year before falling again by year's end. Up and down, up and down, until 2009 when the year ended up 26 percent.

All those market ups and downs over time could result in a volatility-adjusted return—of a little over $3.7 million. Those are annual return figures. Quarterly figures would actually lead to a more volatility-adjusted return.

The point is that market volatility erodes a significant amount: in my example, around $1.6 million of the return.

At the same time, the money is being exposed to taxation. That's basically in thirds: one-third each to long-term gains, short-term gains, and unrealized taxes. In other words, everything in the portfolio is not taxed every single year, nor is it all taxed at the same rate.

For instance, as I write this book, short-term gains and ordinary dividends are taxed at 37 percent, which is the current top marginal tax bracket. Qualified dividends and long-term capital gains are taxed at 20 percent. On the $400,000 portfolio that I just mentioned, taxes eroded it to around $1.9 million.

Guess what else? That's all being impacted by inflation, college expenses, underinsured property, and all the other pressures I mentioned at the beginning of the chapter. And that doesn't even factor in investment management fees. If expenses on that same portfolio were 2 percent, that would drive $1.9 million down to about $1.2 million. That's why spreadsheets are killing you—because your wealth is under attack. You cannot look only at the good side of all the numbers that you are adding up. You cannot ignore financial pressures, or you will be left with less wealth. I talk a lot more about how pressures are eroding your wealth and other points of wealth management in my book *5 Ways Your Wealth Is Under Attack*.

DON'T GET STUCK IN THE GAP

Strategic Coach® Dan Sullivan has a concept known as "The Gap™"
that looks at how people measure their goals against what they view
as the ideal outcome. He says we can measure progress through measurable goals as we reach toward the future we want to achieve.[2]

Having measurable goals and a realistic view are important to
success with a financial strategy. Part of that strategy includes understanding and minimizing the impact of market volatility on your
money.

Minimizing market volatility is easier said than done, consider-
ing that the unpredictability of the stock market can surprise even
the most seasoned investors. One way to make a little sense of it all
is to know the difference between average rate of return, sequence of
returns, and actual return. *Average rate of return* is the average rate of
return over the life of an investment. *Sequence of returns* is the order
in which your investments provide you with a return. *Actual return* is
the actual amount of money gained or lost during a quarter or year
compared to the initial value of an investment.

Using some very simple examples: After one year, an average rate
of return of 25 percent on a $100,000 portfolio would be $125,000;
at the end of year two, about $156,250. Using sequence of returns,
a portfolio of $100,000 might go up by 100 percent in the first year,
resulting in $200,000. However, if that were to fall 50 percent, it
would be back down to $100,000, leaving you with an actual return
of—0 percent. And that's before taxes and fees.

The problem is that these all boil down to one thing—a focus
on returns, or what's known in the industry as the "Rate of Return

---

2   Dan Sullivan, "How to Measure Your Success," *Strategic Coach*, accessed August
     31, 2019, https://resources.strategiccoach.com/the-multiplier-mindset-blog/
     how-to-measure-your-success.

Olympics." Investment managers, Wall Street, financial planners, mutual fund salesmen, ETFs, RIAs—everybody's in this race. Who's got the best rate of return?

Every year, *Money* magazine posts top-performing mutual funds for the year. All the money goes into those funds, and then it either meets the investor's expectations or it doesn't. What really happens is what's reported every year by Dalbar.[3] In 2017, the average equity mutual fund investor underperformed the S&P 500 by about 4.7 percent. Although there were 11.96 percent gains in the broader market, the average investor only saw a 7.26 percent return. The twenty-year S&P 500 annualized return was 7.68 percent. But the average return for equity fund investors was 4.79 percent. That's a 2.89 percent gap.

What the Dalbar study reveals is that people are chasing returns. They buy an asset class, or they buy a fund based on its past performance. It doesn't do well, they sell it, they buy the next hot-performing fund. Over the years, the hot asset class has changed. In 2004 through 2007, for instance, emerging markets went up and down between second-best and best performer, hovering between 26 percent and 40 percent. Then, in 2008, emerging markets dropped 53 percent; if you had $100,000 in emerging markets, you'd have $47,000 after it dropped. But if you were to be heartsick and sell, then you'd really lose out because the next year, emerging markets were back on top again, at 79 percent.

> AS LONG AS YOU CHASE RETURNS, YOU WILL FALL INTO THE HUGE TRAP THAT JUST KEEPS ERODING PEOPLE'S WEALTH.

---

3   Lance Roberts, "Opinion: Americans are still terrible at investing, annual study once again shows," MarketWatch, October 21, 2017, accessed March 24, 2019, https://www.marketwatch.com/story/americans-are-still-terrible-at-investing-annual-study-once-again-shows-2017-10-19.

As long as you chase returns, you will fall into the huge trap that just keeps eroding people's wealth.

Financial success does not come from chasing returns or selecting a magic product or asset class. It comes from having a balanced plan, and then stress testing that plan for weak areas to see how taxes, fees, inflation, obsolescence, technological changes, lawsuits, disability, medical expenses, interest rates, market volatility, college costs, risk, and so many other variables can impact your wealth potential.

My own father is an example of how planning and stress testing can help you prepare for life's unexpected challenges. We had been partners in the business for twenty-five years. Then, at age seventy-one, he decided he wanted to go to Florida for six months, leaving me and the staff to take care of the business. He was gone twenty-two days when he fell and broke his back in three places. He spent ninety days in an ICU facility and then ended up in hospice. Three years later, he's out of hospice, but he's disabled—he's done working.

During that unfortunate time in our lives, my mother and I were walking into the hospital, and I realized that, after all the planning, we would be executing all the protection measures we had put in place over the years. Thanks to all the planning, everything was protected: my father's wealth, my mother, me (his only child), and the business. We had a plan that included the potential for really bad shit happening—and it worked.

That's because he had created a financial plan that looked at real financial pressures and continued to test it over time.

A PLAN BASED ON YOUR WEALTH CURVE

Most financial planners ask how much money you have to invest and how much you can put away monthly. That's it. Or they may not even talk to you unless you have a million dollars to invest. It doesn't matter how much income you make or how many assets you've accumulated—we're going to talk to you; we're going to help you build your wealth. One of the largest clients my father and I worked with came to us when he didn't have much money. He had some credit card debt and was just starting to build his own business. We created a plan with him, and he proceeded to build a very successful business. Over time, he accumulated a lot of wealth and didn't even need the business sale in order to retire; that just added gravy to the deal. We've got a wonderful relationship because it was a team approach all the way. If we had told him, "Oh, you don't have enough money. Come back to us when you do," he would have gone to someone else, and we would have never had the opportunity to work with him. To me, the fun and excitement is in the building, in going through all the ups and downs together.

No two clients are the same, but we typically work with three types of clients: corporate executives, owners of small to midsize businesses, or individuals who are successful in life, but whose portfolios are on the brink of disaster. It's very common for us to find that, while many clients are financially successful, they're not maximizing their wealth and their wealth's potential. Whatever the circumstances, we create a plan tailored to your situation using a wealth management process based on your Wealth Curve. The Wealth Curve concept came about after I joined my father in business. He had already been in business for more than twenty years at that time and had seen a tremendous amount of change in the economy and markets, from hyperinflation to high interest rates to a ten-year treasury at 15.81 percent.

In spite of all this volatility, the industry likes to make the math fairly simple: you have a certain amount of money, you have a certain amount of time to hit your goal, and there are certain assumptions on the return that you can make. There you are—happy retirement.

That's just not how it works. You don't know if you have the time. Everything changes, and the result is consistent pressure on your wealth. I had already been talking with clients about all this for a few years when I gave a presentation to a group of financial advisors about the concept of timeline. The conversation at that time was geared toward life insurance as part of a financial plan.

I broke the presentation down into three components from when I started in the industry and to where I was at that time. What resulted was an exponential curve. Over the life of the curve, the life insurance took on many different roles, moving from wealth accumulation into enjoyment of the wealth to passing the wealth on.

About a week after I gave the presentation, Hurricane Sandy devastated the area of New Jersey where I live. For thirteen days, we had no electricity, so the office was essentially closed down. After a few days, I managed to get a generator for my home, so we had limited electricity there but not enough to power the internet all day long. With more time on my hands, I took the opportunity every morning to sit down with my daughter's unused sketch book and colored pens and pencils and draw out different financial simulations on a curve. I got up every morning and sat there for two or three hours just writing and thinking, writing and thinking. I literally wrote out and planned every financial scenario I could think of, and that became the financial pressures I've been talking about.

That led to the creation of the Wealth Curve concept, which

became the basis for the wealth management process that we use. The process involves sitting down with you and really understanding your circumstances, pressures, and goals; putting together a plan—a blueprint, as you'll discover; stress testing that blueprint; implementing it; and then upgrading it annually to ensure you continue to be on track with your goals.

The process works for people at any age. We've got clients in their nineties who update their plans every year. Just like there's no magic investment or financial product, there's no magic age of retirement. Very wealthy, very successful people often don't retire. They change their job roles—they do less of what they hate doing and more of what they love to do. Bill Gates is not retired; he's doing something that he loves and is still growing money. He still has an impact on his company.

Unfortunately, there are people who hate their jobs, and in truth, their companies won't let them stay past a certain age. If you're in that situation and woefully underprepared, then the next five years mean making some significant changes—that starts with changing your plan right now.

Even if you're already retired, you can have a better outcome with a better plan. One of my really great clients referred us to his parents.

THAT'S OUR JOB—TO PROVIDE CONFIDENCE AND CLARITY AND TAKE THE PRESSURE OFF.

They were already retired for about ten years at that time, and they had been subject to market volatility, inflation, and a lot of pressure. They had been calling their son, my client, and talking about how they were afraid they were going to run out of money. We worked with the parents and developed a plan that put some guaranteed income in place, balanced other areas, and took all the pressure away. After that, instead of all the conversations centering around the ups and downs of the market, all they talk about is the dad's golf game.

That's our job—to provide confidence and clarity and take the pressure off.

Going through the Wealth Curve process will help you understand where you are and whether you are going to get where you want to go.

REMEMBER:

- You are the most important part of your financial plan. Your ability to earn income and save money impacts your entire world.

- Factors are applying pressure to your finances, preventing your Wealth Curve from growing exponentially.

- To be successful, you need to factor all of the financial pressures into your plan.

- The "magic" that is going to save your retirement is to put together multiple products and multiple strategies in an integrated way that is unique to you, the individual.

- Market volatility erodes a significant amount of wealth.

- As long as you chase returns, you will fall into a trap that will erode your wealth.

CHAPTER TWO

THE WEALTH CURVE PROCESS–THE BLUEPRINT FOR SUCCESS

When it comes to wealth planning, everybody's got an opinion, everybody's got a bias. Accountants say one thing, mutual fund advisors say another, stockbrokers and life insurance agents say something else. Even your brother-in-law tends to weigh in. But most people don't think big picture.

Instead of just selling people financial products, I want clients to have a strategy, a plan. Strategy first, products later. That plan should be reviewed and updated on an annual basis. That's the way to ensure a more predictable financial future is in the cards.

That plan will identify problems, help you understand those problems, and reveal why and where changes need to be made. It will help you gain by reducing taxes and reducing risk. It will have lower fees and costs. It will give you more benefits and more protection. Ideally, it will save more money, increase your retirement income, and increase the inheritance to your family. If you're not getting those benefits from a financial strategy, why bother having one?

These are the reasons that I developed a wealth management process based on the Wealth Curve. There are multiple components to the process, the first of which is the Wealth Curve Conversation using the Wealth Curve Pressure Identifier.

THE WEALTH CURVE CONVERSATION AND PRESSURE IDENTIFIER

The Wealth Curve Conversation was designed to help you understand the impact financial pressures have on your wealth and its potential. Through the conversation, we get to the heart of your financial situation.

To help us organize the data that we gather from the conversation, we use what we call the Wealth Curve Pressure Identifier. The Wealth Curve Pressure Identifier is designed to capture unique dynamics and create a snapshot of your family makeup and elements of your financial life, including income, tax structure, savings rate, debt structure, and even lifestyle. This information helps form the initial building blocks of a wealth plan.

Let me explain why each of these dynamics is important and some potential impacts they may have.

Family. The key to a successful wealth plan is not just the numbers. What matters is the family dynamics—spouse, ex-spouses, children, parents, siblings, and in-laws. The family dynamics are probably the least discussed part of a financial plan. But they should be the most important part because the steps you take toward your goals are determined by those dynamics.

We use the conversation and pressure identifier to understand the unique dynamics of the mix of people who are coming together because people are assets—and they are liabilities. Through this first step of the process, we often find that, in many big families, one person is very secure, but others in the family in some way rely on that person. If that person is you, it can mean a lot of financial pressure.

For instance, if you are the sole provider and have children, then expenses may include putting them through college, hosting their sweet sixteens or bar mitzvahs, buying their first cars, or paying for a wedding or two.

We also want to know about parents and siblings. We look at their ages and their health. If they are deceased, did they leave liabilities? Did they leave an estate, and if so, is that money protected? If an inheritance is in your future, we want to see protections in place to ensure the money reaches its intended destination very easily when the time comes.

One example of the impact of an inheritance might be if a sole provider father were to receive a $1 million inheritance when he had three high schoolers. That million dollars might seem like he was all set to finance their college educations. But if the money is not set up in a trust or a vehicle such as a 529 College Savings Plan, he could easily find it all taken away by a divorce or creditors of his business. And since that inheritance would increase the family income, there's a real chance that it would negate the kids' chances for financial aid.

Income. Everyone has income and assets. The majority of people have less than $50,000 in the bank, and they have more in qualified and nonqualified assets. Where most balance sheets fall down is by looking only at income. We want to look not only at the income, but also at all of the liabilities and future liabilities. We want to know not only the current situation, but also how assets and interests will determine income and cover your obligations in the future.

Taxes. Most people do not know what they really pay in federal or state taxes. They don't know what's going to Medicare and FICA. If we look at the income and understand where the taxes are, we can begin to find strategies for reducing the amount of income that shows up on a tax return, but still getting money back and still growing the wealth. More than just looking at tax avoidance strategies, we're looking at balance.

Savings. What percentage of income are you actually saving? For some, it's a lot. For others, not so much.

When we look at where the savings are, we see whether it's savings through debt reduction, through savings accounts, or through some sort of opportunity fund. Then, where is that savings going? If it's going to a retirement plan, we want to know whether any available employer match is being maximized. Are the savings being built up in life insurance cash values or annuities? Or maybe it's a stock purchase plan through work where you're buying company shares at a discount?

> **WHEN IT COMES TO SAVINGS, IT DOESN'T MATTER WHERE IT'S OCCURRING INITIALLY. IT'S ALL ABOUT THE HABIT ITSELF.**

Savings on income tax is one of the most important parts of a plan. If we drop taxes from 31 percent to 29 percent and move that 2 percent difference over to savings, the amount of wealth you create over a twenty-five or thirty-year period can make all the difference in retirement.

When it comes to savings, it doesn't matter where it's occurring initially. It's all about the habit itself. I recently met with a client's son who was in his late twenties. Dad had a great habit of saving, and the son had fortunately inherited that habit. He didn't really know what he was doing, but when we put together his Wealth Curve Blueprint (which I'll talk about next), we determined that he was actually saving 38 percent of his income. That's powerful. At age twenty-seven, he was actually way ahead of schedule, and it was a real point of pride that he had accumulated so much wealth on his own, and without really sacrificing lifestyle. But he knew that savings rate couldn't continue forever—he knew it would change once he married and had kids. I'll talk more about savings rates in the next chapter.

Debt structure. Debt can include everything from credit cards to car loans, mortgages to student loans. The key with debt is to look at how it is structured. Is the cash flow optimal? Paying off debt is a form of savings, but if it's done the wrong way, you won't have enough liquidity. Debt structure also includes income taxes—are you getting the best tax benefits for the debt structure that you have?

Lifestyle. Income minus savings minus debt should equal lifestyle: out of one dollar earned, you pay thirty cents in taxes and save fifteen cents. Some of what's left goes to debt. The rest should equal lifestyle. But if part of that debt is a credit card, then you're probably spending more than you're earning. Stuff happens. Things unexpectedly break, and without enough liquidity, you've got $5,000 on the credit card.

I personally believe that the concept in financial planning that says you're going to need 70 percent of your current income in retirement is a fallacy. Why do I question that? Because when you're working, you're putting in forty or more hours a week at a job. You're not out spending money on your lifestyle activities; you're putting in time to earn money. At retirement, suddenly there's forty or more hours to fill—and all those hours won't be spent earning at the same rate you did when you were working. So it's not unrealistic to believe that you might actually need even more money in retirement.

The mindset that we need less in retirement creates an excuse for people. It keeps people from thinking about saving enough money. It keeps them from a maximum perspective. They don't think about questions like "How do I really want to spend my retirement?" Most people don't want to sit at home all day and watch CNBC; most want something more—they want to travel, to do things with their kids and grandkids, to contribute to charities. Most of what they want to do will cost money.

Down the road, everything is going to cost more. Food will cost more, vacations will cost more, life will cost more. As I write this, I've got one child out of college and two kids in college. I can remember holding each child and wanting that child to be as successful as they possibly could. Even back then I knew that if my child wanted to go to Harvard, then my financial plan should support their dreams because that's what I wanted as well. But all those future outflows that I mentally or verbally committed to were going to put pressure on my plan. Whether it's a second home, a boat, a supervacation, or a family milestone, all of those are future goals.

When setting up a plan, you have to decide how to position the money today so that it actually provides you with the same or more income, inflation adjusted, moving forward. Having tools that track your spending can help you have a very clear understanding of how your dollars come and go on a monthly basis, providing a realistic picture of where you are and can potentially be. That's how to avoid finding out five years away from retirement that instead of spending $10,000 per month, you're actually spending $12,000 per month.

I can't stress enough the importance of having an optimal balance between all of the components of a wealth plan. It can be done, but it must be intentional—and it must be done now, not five years from now, not five years from retirement. If you're not aware of the numbers— where you're spending and saving money, how your debt is structured, how you can reduce taxes—then you're not going to get to where you want to go.

> " I CAN'T STRESS ENOUGH THE IMPORTANCE OF HAVING AN OPTIMAL BALANCE BETWEEN ALL OF THE COMPONENTS OF A WEALTH PLAN. IT CAN BE DONE, BUT IT MUST BE INTENTIONAL— AND IT MUST BE DONE NOW, NOT FIVE YEARS FROM NOW, NOT FIVE YEARS FROM RETIREMENT.

With a lifestyle checkup, we can see what to modify today to make for a better retirement tomorrow. That might mean increasing savings, decreasing taxes, making debts more efficient, modifying some of what you're paying for today but not really enjoying.

For instance, by looking at margin of utility, a measure called UTIL, we can see how much enjoyment you're getting for the things you're spending money on. What expenses do you have that are not adding value? If the UTIL is low—the expense outweighs the enjoyment you're getting from it—then why do it? If you're paying $19.99 per month for a streaming service but never use it, what is your level of enjoyment for that expense? Zero. That's a very small example, but multiply that by month after month of nonuse, or multiple similar services never used, and it can be hundreds of dollars a month—thousands of dollars every year. I've seen clients' budgets with hundreds of dollars a month of items that they had no idea they were spending money on, services they signed up for and then just forgot about. There are so many subscription-based models out there today, and they're all automatically charged to the credit card. Just pay the bill each month and move on, never questioning the balance on the card until it tips the scale.

Too often, people are spending money on stuff and don't even know they're doing it. Streaming TV, high cable bills, all the little extras that they signed up for over the years—and never use. Getting rid of those things can put a lot of money back into a budget. The same goes for interest costs, finance charges, and other kinds of fees. All of those are pressures that erode wealth.

I have clients making a million dollars a year that are having trouble saving 5 or 10 percent of that wealth. Why? Because of their financial pressures. In some cases, it's poor habits—they haven't paid attention to their money. By being really smart, we can minimize erosion of wealth and move the money over to savings. Over time, that can help grow a 5 or 6 percent savings rate to 10 or 15 percent— or more. You can't do it overnight, but you can do it over time. But you need to know those deficiencies today so that you can begin to make changes now, not ten or fifteen years from now. Not when you're ready to retire.

The Wealth Curve Conversation using the Pressure Identifier can help you begin to understand the truth about your situation. And that truth is visually represented in what we call the Wealth Curve Blueprint.

THE WEALTH CURVE BLUEPRINT

The Wealth Curve Blueprint was formulated because we didn't want to just have conversations with clients to tell them "everything's rosy," when it isn't. We wanted to be realistic and help them understand how they were going to be impacted by the decisions they were making about their wealth.

We designed the Wealth Curve Blueprint to be a snapshot of your present plan—where you are right now. With the blueprint, all financial decisions made over the last twenty-five years or more come together in one place to provide a macro view of your current situation. However, it is not designed to be a road map for where you're going or a history of where you've been. It is a current, at-a-glance view of the most important parts of your plan: family makeup, income sources, savings rate, taxes, mortgages and debts, property taxes, insurance payments, lifestyle, and more.

The blueprint is one of the most important components to a financial plan because it reveals all the components unique to your circumstances and financial pressures. It uses data collected during the conversation to reveal whether your Wealth Curve is trending up or down. It shows whether your financial pressure is too high, there's too much volatility, you're overspending or undersaving, you don't have enough protection against a lawsuit or disability—all the components that can impact your plan. It is designed to help you understand, identify, and rank, in the order of potential risk, the forces attacking your wealth.

Once everything is organized into the blueprint, then we can begin to look at strategies to reduce taxes, fees, and costs and to increase savings rate. It also lets us see how well your plan is protected, and it gives us a big-picture view of your lifestyle so we can look at ways to modify it moving forward. We can even see whether credit card debt, tax debt, or business liabilities are going to impact your personal plan; then we can use that information to work on debt structure.

More than most balance sheets, which typically show current assets and liabilities, the blueprint also considers future obligations—and all those future "wants" in life. Whether it's a supervacation for the family, paying for college or weddings, or giving to charities, by seeing your current situation in the blueprint, all those future obligations can be captured and made part of your wealth plan.

For instance, we might see that you're putting away $25,000 a year in anticipation of spending $300,000 to fund your kids' college educations. But is that the most efficient use of that money? And if you put your kids through college, will there still be enough money to retire? These are questions to be asked and then answered as part of your wealth plan.

Let's look at sample clients John and Molly Redbank. The dynamics of their family include living parents, siblings, and any relatives who might be a financial burden or who might leave inheritance money. John and Molly have two children, Junior and Kayla, so the couple's information includes future expenses for college and weddings. We may also need to include in their plan milestone birthdays for the kids or cars that need to be purchased. By creating a blueprint for them, we can see how they earn their money, where the money is invested, and the contributions being made. We can see their residences (primary and secondary), debt structure (credit cards, mortgages, and rental properties), and protection and defense (life insurance, disability insurance, long-term care, will, and trusts).

By having everything captured on a blueprint, John and Molly can be aware of all their pressures, and we can begin to identify and overcome the financial leaks in their plan. Let me explain what I mean by financial leaks, because fixing those leaks in your plan can make a significant difference in the long term.

Take a term life insurance policy, for instance, with a yearly premium of $1,000 when paid annually. Typically, the insurance company offers several convenient ways to pay for such a policy, including monthly premiums of, say, $87. The trouble with those convenient payments is they actually make the annual premium total $1,044. Over thirty years, with no rate increase, that's $1,320 extra just for the convenience of paying monthly. That $1,320 convenience fee is equal to more than a whole year's worth of coverage.

Factor that kind of math across your plan—convenience fees on insurance for your car, house, life; fees to banking institutions; late fees on credit cards—and we may find hundreds or thousands of dollars in excess fees in a single year. Let's say, for instance, we find $1,800 in excess charges in a single year. Investing that $1,800 in a way that it earns 5 percent interest over twenty-five years could return $85,000. If you plan to be on the planet another fifty years, that return could reach $376,000. Those are convenience fees you're paying someone else. That's what I mean by leaks in your plan—and believe me, there are leaks all over your plan.

Once we have your specific metrics and can see everything on your blueprint, then we can start to determine whether meeting your goals is realistic, and we can begin to make any needed modifications.

That's where the value of the next component comes in: the Wealth Curve Scorecard.

THE WEALTH CURVE SCORECARD

The Wealth Curve Scorecard looks at formulas to determine whether you are on track with your financial goals. It's based on approximately twenty performance indicators ranging from debt liability and college savings to future liabilities and lifestyle scale. It lets us see very quickly whether you are in good (green) or bad (red) standing with the current situation.

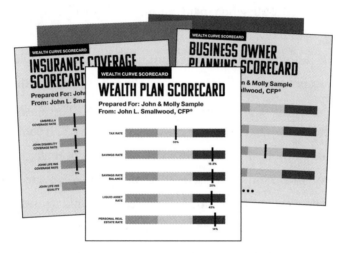

One of the key indicators on the scorecard is savings rate. For instance, if you are forty-five years old and making $350,000 a year, at this stage of life, your savings rate should be north of 20 percent. Without meeting that standard, you're probably not going to accumulate enough money to retire at the same level of lifestyle unless a lightning bolt of wealth comes out of left field.

But if you're like the majority of people, you have to accumulate wealth in order to retire. All too often, we encounter people three to four years away from retirement whose income is going from $400,000 to $150,000. While $150,000 may sound nice, it is quite an adjustment after living off $400,000. We recommend that when making less than $100,000 in salary, you should be saving at least 10 percent, and that figure should grow as income grows. The next chapter is an in-depth look at savings rates and the value of saving on a wealth plan.

John and Molly's scorecard let us know they were in the red where their savings toward their goal was concerned. Their retirement goal was to accumulate $3 million, but with only fifteen years left to retirement, they only had $500,000 saved.

We can invest that $500,000 and rely on rate of return, but that's not going to make them successful in their retirement—a higher rate of return will not make up for all their undersaving. Rates of return are not guarantees. Volatility makes rate of return too unpredictable. When I started my business in the late 1980s, I could get a 6 or 7 percent return on a money market fund. One million dollars in the bank would earn $70,000 a year in interest. Compounded over twenty years, I should have $5,427,000 before taxes and before inflation. But the interest rates have collapsed since then. Here, at the other end of that wonderful financial world, we're happy if we get a rate of 2.5 percent.

Instead, we know that increasing their savings rate is more likely to make them successful, to help them reach their goals. If they're only putting away $20,000 a year in a 401(k), and they need another $100,000 to be where they should be, then they are overspending somewhere.

At this point, we would refer back to their blueprint, where we would likely find that budget is the problem. Their plan may allow for $10,000 spending per month in retirement, but at this point, they're actually spending $13,000. Mathematically, their spending is 30 percent higher than they think, so a $10,000-per-month plan boils down to denial. Either the plan must change, or the spending must change. It's that simple.

That's why plans based purely on assumptions are frickin' wrong—yet those are the kinds of plans so many people have. Even with the blueprint, we make certain assumptions. Your income will continue to increase every year by a certain percentage rate, you're going to keep saving at a healthy rate, your employer is going to put in a contribution, and taxes and fees are going to stay static. We can even assume certain rates of return and that you're going to be able to keep working. But again, those are assumptions. The only guarantee I can make is that everything I just ticked off is going to change. And so will your plan.

As part of the Wealth Curve process, we expose your plan to different strategies and different financial pressures. That's where the Wealth Curve Simulation comes in.

THE WEALTH CURVE SIMULATION

Once we create your blueprint and review your Wealth Curve Scorecard, then we can begin to stress test factors that are crucial to the success of your plan. We can create certain assumptions to see whether everything will actually happen as planned. In short, we look at all the variables I mentioned at the beginning of chapter one. We look at all those pressures that are impacting your Wealth Curve because we know that, from day to day, they're going to change.

With the Wealth Curve Simulation, we create different scenarios such as what will happen if

- interest rates drop;

- there's market volatility;

- you become disabled;

- there's a long-term-care event;

- you get sued; or

- your pension doesn't pay off as planned.

By creating different scenarios, we can see whether, for instance, a 31 percent savings rate that seems adequate really is. Most people only save 5 or 6 percent and think that will help them retire. They put $20,000 into their 401(k) and ignore all the other variables that are putting pressure on their wealth. They don't realize that all those pressures are preventing them from getting to their goal.

As I was writing this book, I went skiing in Colorado, and on the last day there, it snowed—a lot. One of the heaviest snows of the season. And every one of those snowflakes was unique. Each had its own distinct story to tell. Each of them was also destined to melt, to deteriorate. Well, that's your financial plan. It's your own unique story, but it's destined to change and potentially deteriorate unless you review it every year.

When we annually apply simulations, we can see what changed and what to do about it to keep your plan from deteriorating. By using the simulator, we can apply all the pressures and see whether it's all adding up to a successful retirement in the future.

Over time, your roles, your responsibilities, and your goals will evolve. Why shouldn't your financial plan also evolve? It shouldn't be tossed in a drawer and never visited again. It should be reviewed on a regular basis so that all the changing variables can be taken into account. A regular review can help you understand what has changed in your dynamics every year. Corporate benefits change. Business climates change. Interest rates, expenses, lifestyles, family dynamics—all of these change, and all of those changes affect a financial plan.

HONESTY AND GOOD HABITS LEAD TO SUCCESS

Often, someone new to the Wealth Curve will comment that they need a certain amount, say $10,000, per month just to fund their lifestyle. That's $120,000 a year. They're making $300,000 per year, paying about $75,000 in taxes, and putting $20,000 into their 401(k) plan. All told, that leaves $85,000 unaccounted for. Where's that money going? If it's not in a savings account or other asset class, then they're spending it. Divide that $85,000 by twelve; that's an additional $7,000 per month over the $10,000 that the individual reportedly needs to fund their lifestyle. If we build a plan that will provide $10,000 per month in retirement, but that individual really needs $17,000, that plan's not going to work.

The Wealth Curve management process is about understanding where you are now and what we can do to improve your retirement numbers. That's why you must be very clear on where you are and use good information—not half information, not half truths—when building and updating your plan. By working through the Wealth Curve system, we can build a really good plan based on your current situation, execute that plan, and then see where you are in twelve months. Then, without blame or excuses, you can accept the facts about your situation and figure out what to do moving forward.

Building a long-term strategy takes time. The only way to make improvements is to understand where you are to start with and then create good habits that you can stick to for long-term success. One of the best habits you can make is to adopt a healthy savings rate.

REMEMBER:

- Strategy first, products later.

- A wealth plan should identify problems and reveal why and where changes need to be made.

- The plan should be reviewed and updated on an annual basis.

- The Wealth Curve Conversation gets to the heart of your financial situation.

- The Wealth Curve Pressure Identifier helps organize your data.

- The Wealth Curve Blueprint is a snapshot of your present plan.

- The Wealth Curve Scorecard uses performance indicators to determine whether you are on track with your financial goals.

- The Wealth Curve Simulator creates assumptions to see whether your plan will work.

CHAPTER THREE

SAVINGS RATE AND RATE OF RETURN

When it comes to creating a stronger wealth plan, there is perhaps no greater power than savings rate. The biggest gauge of financial success in retirement is not how much money you have. It is understanding how you spend what you have in retirement. And savings rate is the fuel that's going to get you there. Undersaving leads to overspending. And if that's been a habit your entire life, why would you change in retirement?

In this chapter, I'm going to discuss savings rate largely as a simple equation: saving more means a better chance of success in retirement. Most of my discussion won't include the pressures on your financial plan, which ultimately affect your savings rate. If you keep everything within certain ratios, then you'll have a greater chance of success.

That's why the greater your savings rate, the higher the probability of reaching your goals.

However, while every percentage increase in savings rate improves your chances of success, it can also mean a drop in lifestyle. Make no mistake: I'm a big fan of enjoying money that we earn, but that enjoyment must be within the lifestyle restraints of our income. And it must factor in rate of savings. That's tough for a lot of people to do. Some people want to drive a big, prestigious car, but that big car also comes with a big opportunity cost—all the extra money that car costs is taking away from savings or money that can be earned on savings toward a more successful retirement. On the flip side, I've also seen people who are saving too much money, and they're not enjoying life at all. These people are not recognizing a key point: it's only going to take their kids a few years to spend everything that it's taken them fifty years to save.

It's your money. You can do what you want with it. As a wealth advisor, I really can't make you stop spending it how you like. But as a Certified Financial Planner, I have a fiduciary responsibility to give good financial advice. And part of that is getting really good facts. That starts by being truthful with yourself. If you make $250,000 a year, give $50,000 of that to the government in taxes, and then spend the rest without saving anything, at some point that's going to lead to a financial breakdown. If the current you is spending every dime you make, the future you is going to be pretty upset—do you really want to live with a future you who knows you should have taken control of your finances earlier?

I'm guilty of overspending myself, and I understand how it happens. I'm in a volatile industry where I earn money, sometimes a lot of money, and then I don't. Life happens; I get it. But if I find out during the Wealth Curve Conversation that someone has $30,000 of credit card debt, I'm going to ask what happened and why. Usually, I find out it's because someone overspent. If you have a set salary and you're overspending, then there's a problem. If you have a bonus structure that fluctuates—one year it's a monster, then next year it's practically nil—and you're overspending, then there's a problem. Once we see the problem, then we have to figure out how to fix it moving forward. If it's because of a repeating pattern of overspending, then it may be a problem that's beyond the scope of a financial advisor.

WHAT IS YOUR DREAM FOR YOUR FINANCIAL FUTURE? HELPING YOU GET THERE IS OUR SUPERPOWER.

That's why we build a blueprint and then stress test it. We want to see whether your savings rate is appropriate. Will the money you're accumulating based on current goals realistically meet your future goals? A good financial advisor will help see whether you are really on track, or will be the bearer of bad news if you're not. They will also tell you whether you are putting too much pressure on yourself. What is your dream for your financial future? Helping you get there is our superpower.

Here are some of the fundamentals of saving that we impress on every client:

Think of yourself as a business. Savings is a way to invest in yourself, so think of yourself as a business. If you want to keep regenerating yourself, investing in your future, then putting in more than 5 or 6 percent is the way to be successful.

A healthy savings rate can help when the unexpected happens. A savings rate is not only about putting away money for retirement. It's also about putting away money for the unexpected in life. I have an old Victorian house that I have to keep fixing all the time. If I put off repairs instead of fixing them when they happen, then it will cost me more money in the long run to keep up the house. It's the same with savings—stay on top of it with a healthy savings rate, and you'll be less likely to have to play catch-up later on.

The more saved, the more wealth grows over time. If you're not putting away a certain amount of money every single year as a percentage of your salary, then pressures are actually going to push you backward. There are tried-and-true formulas for establishing a healthy savings rate, and they can be tailored to your family's needs. For instance, we recommend that when you're making less than $100,000 in salary, you should be saving at least 10 percent, and that figure should grow as your income grows.

This is a simple breakdown of suggested savings rates.

- <$99,999.99: 10 percent

- <$199,999.99: 15 percent of $100,000

- <$499,999.99: 20 percent of $300,000

- <$999,999.99: 25 percent of $500,000

- >$1 million: 30 percent

Most people don't really know where their money is going. They can't account for the dollars they are spending and can't believe what they're being told about their future in the face of their poor rate of savings. But once they do the math themselves, they'll often come back and tell me, "You're right; I actually am spending that amount of money. I had no idea."

EVERY DOLLAR COUNTS

Very frequently, when we look at a client's savings rate, we find that most of their wealth is in their 401(k) plan. With our corporate executive clients, who are often individuals who draw a salary and bonuses, we often find that all their wealth is in stock options and long-term incentives that they expect to sell at some point to capture wealth. In fact, especially with high-level corporate individuals, it's all too common to see their entire portfolio tied to the company.

The problem with everything being in a 401(k) or in big stock options is that there's a risk of losing everything. We've all seen a stock that was flying high and then plummeted. Lucent Technologies is a great example of that. People whose entire 401(k) was invested in company stock lost millions of dollars when the company imploded. There's a laundry list of companies that are examples of that. Of course, there's another list of companies that went the opposite direction—nowhere but up, and still rising.

There's another problem with having no cash or other investments outside a 401(k) plan or company stock: liquidity. People who have all their savings tied up in their 401(k) frequently have taken loans on the money or have credit card debt because they have no available cash.

When you save your dollars, those dollars should not be located in one asset. Instead of having all of your eggs in a 401(k) or in company stock, we can show you how to diversify into broader strategies to create a balanced asset class through multiple types of savings vehicles with more than one tax structure. Every dollar you save should be building up your liquid savings, short- and long-term savings, and defensive savings, which should allocate your dollars to different types of tax structures. We can also systematically take money off the table and reposition it into risk-reduction strategies. The goal is to have multiple sources of retirement income. That way, if any one or more sources dries up, or changes in tax law turn a gusher of a strategy into a trickle, then you will still be able to enjoy a comfortable lifestyle.

While it's superimportant to understand the role of every dollar that you have in a plan, budgets don't really work, because life happens. But if you put your savings rate first, ultimately it really doesn't matter where you spend the rest.

> BUDGETS DON'T REALLY WORK, BECAUSE LIFE HAPPENS. BUT IF YOU PUT YOUR SAVINGS RATE FIRST, ULTIMATELY IT REALLY DOESN'T MATTER WHERE YOU SPEND THE REST.

Here are just a few areas of your plan and how they should be structured to help you have the most efficient savings rate:

Liquid savings. Liquid savings is money that is available to you without surrender charges and that is free of market volatility. By having around 50 percent of your annual expenses in liquid cash reserves, you'll have access to funds when you need them.

Short- and long-term savings. Short-term savings should be allocated to cash, savings, checking, short-term bonds, and whole life cash value. Long-term savings should be allocated to bonds, stock, real estate, IRAs, 401(k)s, and Roth plans.

Defensive savings. Approximately 10 percent of your invested assets should be in defense strategies, such as disability or long-term care insurance, or a whole life policy with a death benefit.

Lifestyle costs. Back when banks were lending 40 percent, I would go into a client's house and walk into a big, five-thousand-square-foot mansion that was amazing but completely empty. The house had no drapes, rugs, or furniture, other than maybe a Little Tykes set in the great room for the kids. Why? Because the homeowners had put all their money into their house and didn't have any money left for furnishings. Now they want to talk about savings, but they don't even have enough money to protect themselves.

After income tax, savings rate, primary residence, and defense costs, lifestyle costs should not exceed what is left over. For example, if you have $100,000 in income, then it should break down as:

- 20 percent = taxes (FICA, Medicare, state, local)

- 10 percent = savings. The goal with savings is to start small (around 5 percent) and then grow to as much as 20 percent. I'll explain the benefits of higher savings rates in the next section of this chapter.

- 22 percent = residence (principal, interest, real estate taxes). When purchasing a house, you should always have 20 percent down; your mortgage should be a thirty-year fixed; and your principal, interest, and real estate taxes should not exceed 22 percent of your gross income.

- 10 percent = defense (if less than 10 percent, one-half to savings, one-half to lifestyle). Defense includes auto, home, disability insurance, long-term care insurance, life insurance, major medical, and legal.

This breakdown leaves 38 percent of your monthly budget for lifestyle (second homes should fall into this).

These are basic figures for most situations, but let's look at how a higher rate of savings can make all the difference.

HIGHER SAVINGS, LOWER LIFESTYLE = SUCCESS

Let me show you the difference that a higher rate of savings can make. In this example, we'll use four different households with $250,000 in annual income and annual income tax of $49,000. Each household saves a different percentage of its gross income, from 5 percent to 20 percent.

SAVINGS RATE	5 PERCENT	10 PERCENT	15 PERCENT	20 PERCENT
INCOME	$250,000	$250,000	$250,000	$250,000
TAX	$49,000	$49,000	$49,000	$49,000
LIFESTYLE	$188,500	$176,000	$163,500	$151,000
SAVINGS AMOUNT	$12,500	$25,000	$37,500	$50,000

Fig. 3.1: Savings rate.

As you can see in figure 3.1, the household that spends the most on lifestyle ($188,500) saves the least ($12,500). Conversely, the household that saves the most ($50,000) spends the least on lifestyle ($151,000).

Depending on the market, your savings, and your lifestyle, you can live maybe five or ten years in retirement, or you can live forty or fifty years. A plan that has you retiring at sixty-five and living ten years is not really realistic—these days, living much longer than age seventy-five is more common. How will you pay for those extra years?

By simply reducing your lifestyle and increasing your savings rate, you increase the probability of your money lasting—even if you live to age one hundred.

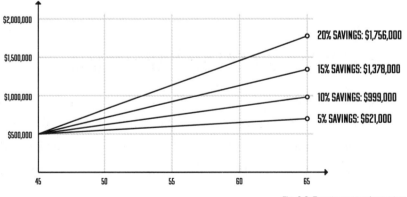

Fig. 3.2: Twenty-year savings rates.

Let's assume that some components in all four households are equal. All of them

- have already saved $500,000;

- are making a 5 percent return;

- are paying 30 percent tax; and

- are forty-five-year-old earners.

All of these components being equal, what sets the households apart over twenty years are the savings rates. The amount of fuel, the amount of money that's going into savings on a regular basis, is what makes all the difference and results in these portfolio totals:

- 5 percent savings = $621,000

- 10 percent savings = $999,000

- 15 percent sa vings = $1,378,000

- 20 percent savings = $1,756,000

Now let's make some assumptions at retirement. At age sixty-five, let's assume the husband and wife each have Social Security, there's a combined pension of $20,000, and that those contribute to a total $74,000 of predictable income coming in annually.

Where this becomes impactful is when figuring out what that withdrawal rate will do to the portfolio over time. Let's say the couple managed to save $1.8 million. If they're conditioned to live at $188,500 a year, and assuming no inflation, then they're looking at approximately a 10 percent withdrawal rate. That's not going to work for the long term. But if they can move from a lifestyle of $188,500 to $163,500 per year, upping their savings rate another 10 percent to 15 percent, or another $25,000 per year, then they could accumulate $1,747,000. That's a 48 percent increase in their wealth. Plus, their withdrawal rate is reduced to 4.3 percent, assuming no other components of their plan.

WITHDRAWAL RATES			
RETIREMENT PORTFOLIO	PREFERRED WITHDRAWAL (3.5%)	WITHDRAWAL TO MATCH LIFESTYLE	REDUCTION OF LIFESTYLE TO HAVE SUCCESSFUL RETIRMENT
A) $1,756,000	$62,000	$77,000 (4.3%)	$15,000/YR | $1,250/MO
B) $1,378,000	$49,000	$87,000 (6.4%)	$40,000/YR | $3,300/MO
C) $99,000	$35,000	$102,000 (10.2%)	$67,000/YR | $5,600/MO
D) 625,000	$22,000	$114,000 (18.2%)	$92,000/YR | $7,600/MO

Fig. 3.3: Withdrawal rates.

By the chart in figure 3.3, you can see that household A has $1,756,000 and is pulling $77,000 to match its lifestyle. This household's probability of the money lasting in retirement is greater because the withdrawal rate is not out of balance. The household in example A above is more prepared for retirement—these retirees are more prepared for other financial pressures that may come their way, and they are not going to have to adjust their lifestyle as much as the household in example D.

Household D only has $625,000 of assets and a lifestyle that pulls $114,000 from the portfolio. If this household's ideal withdrawal of 3.5 percent is $22,000, then these retirees are overwithdrawing their portfolio by $92,000 annually, or $7,600 per month. Household D in this scenario has a huge crisis happening. If these retirees don't adapt and reduce their lifestyle, they're going to run out of money in just a few years.

Similarly, if the preferred withdrawal rate for household A is $62,000, these retirees are also overwithdrawing. But it will be much easier for this household to adjust its lifestyle by $15,000 a year, or $1,250 per month, than it will be for household D, don't you think?

The household with the $188,500 lifestyle preretirement has to withdraw $114,500 from the portfolio in retirement—an 18 percent withdrawal that will never last. The household with the lowest lifestyle only needs to take out $77,000 from its portfolio—a 4.3 percent withdrawal rate. The odds of a 4.3 percent withdrawal rate working are far greater than an 18 percent rate of withdrawal in retirement.

Dropping a lifestyle by 20 percent—from $188,500 to $150,800—is a pretty big adjustment. It might take two or three years to reach that goal. Yet that's a lot better than having to go from $114,000 to $22,800; that's an 80 percent reduction in lifestyle, or finding ways to stop spending $92,000 per year. Still, for many people, that may be what's needed to succeed in retirement if all they've managed to save is $625,000 because of a 5 percent contribution over the years.

If that's all you've managed to save, if your lifestyle has to be reduced that much, then in retirement you're not

- living where you want to live;

- living with people you want to live with;

- eating in restaurants you want to enjoy;

- traveling to places you want to go; or

- enjoying club memberships you want to have.

Again, overspending all the way through the accumulation phase is not going to save enough money for retirement. You just won't have the freedom to live the way you thought you would. The kind of retirement you have starts with savings habits today.

THE FINANCIAL PLANNING FALLACY

*For every complex problem there is an answer
that is clear, simple, and wrong.*

—H. L. Mencken

There are many studies out there that point to ideal rates of withdrawal. One is from Wade D. Pfau, PhD, CFA, who says that, based on current interest rates and market volatility, a reasonable withdrawal rate from a portfolio is about 3.5 percent.[4] If you take out more money than that, the odds of running out of money go up exponentially. BlackRock also did a study that used what's called the Monte Carlo simulation. It shows withdrawal rates of 4 to 8 percent on $1 million with a diversified portfolio. Someone who started withdrawing at an 8 percent withdrawal rate in 1972 would be out of money in eleven years.

If you're going to be retired for twenty-five years and have a portfolio that is 60 percent stocks and 40 percent bonds, a withdrawal rate of 5 percent means you have a 50 to 60 percent probability of running out of money at the end of twenty-five years. If I get on an airplane, and the pilot says there's a 50 to 60 percent probability that I'll make it to my destination, I'm getting the hell off that plane.

Now, a 3.5 percent rate of withdrawal is a good goal, and the graph in figure 3.3 is based on assumptions of that rate of withdrawal.

But the reality is that neither Pfau's nor BlackRock's studies are really accurate. Why? Because their variables are not the same variables that we will have going forward. All of the charts are

---

4   Wade D. Pfau, "Sustainable Retirement Spending with Low Interest Rates: Updating the Trinity Study," Financial Planning Associates, accessed September 1, 2019, https://www.onefpa.org/journal/Pages/AUG15-Sustainable-Retirement-Spending-with-Low-Interest-Rates-Updating-the-Trinity-Study.aspx.

based on assumptions:

- No inflation on your lifestyle

- Income that remains static

- Tax laws that don't change

- At least 5 percent savings every single year

- Zero spending of already accumulated capital

- No college expenses in your future

- No broken furnaces, dishwashers, and so on in your future

Nothing in a financial plan is likely to stay static. Interest rates, tax rates, and market volatility may increase. Planned obsolescence may worsen. Medical expenses may be higher.

Remember that inflation is a government-calculated number. We're told that inflation over the last fifty years is about 4 percent. Although inflation itself was only 1.8 percent in January 2018, energy alone was up 5.9 percent in 2018 over the prior year.

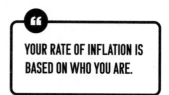

YOUR RATE OF INFLATION IS BASED ON WHO YOU ARE.

The price of food alone has increased by an average of 4.1 percent over fifty years.

Your rate of inflation may be different because it's based on where you live, your buying preferences, and other factors. Your rate of inflation is based on who you are.

Take, for instance, college. There is a difference between the cost of public and private college, and it's increased significantly in forty years. If you were putting a kid through private college in 1975, tuition alone, per semester, cost $3,776 compared to 2015, when it was $42,419. Add room and board to that, and, from my experience, it's closer to $65,000. A postage stamp was thirteen cents in 1975; in

2015, it was forty-nine cents—and they've gone up since then. Back in 1975, a gallon of milk was $1.65; in 2015 it was $3.49.

But here's what's interesting. If you have $100,000 worth of lifestyle today, and inflation is 3 percent, then ten years from now, you will need $130,477 to enjoy the same things you do today.

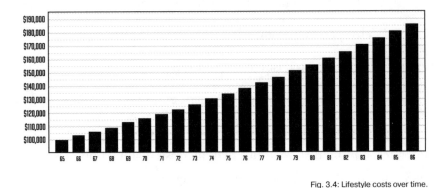

Fig. 3.4: Lifestyle costs over time.

If you don't have a $130,000-plus lifestyle, then your lifestyle will have essentially gone backward. If you retired today and in ten years still had a $100,000 lifestyle, you would actually be spending $73,000 in today's dollars, factoring in inflation, or a 3 percent loss of purchasing power if your income stays flat. How much stuff are you cutting out of your budget over time?

Inflation is one of the pressures that is constantly beating down on your wealth plan. But it's not really something that you can put your finger on, so it's often confused with planned obsolescence and technological change.

Now, I've mentioned planned obsolescence. But what is it exactly? Well, everything you buy is going to wear out and need to be replaced. The roof on your house, your car, the tires and brakes on your car, your refrigerator, your dishwasher. There are style changes— the suit you're wearing today may not be appropriate to wear five years from now. And today, obsolescence also includes cell phones, computers, and operating systems. Breakneck technological changes are costly and must be factored into your plan. In 1990, when I started in the business full time, nobody had a cell phone (except maybe Gordon Gekko from *Wall Street*). Then, everybody had a cell phone. Twenty-five years later, we have cell phones and data plans. Televisions have changed. Everybody's got a Fitbit. All the technology that didn't exist twenty years ago you can't live without today. What's coming tomorrow? Think about all the wonderful crap that we're going to have that we don't have today. Life extension is really taking center stage. Peter Diamandis, with Singularity University, and Ray Kurzweil, the seventy-one-year-old head of Google's artificial intelligence, are predicting that in ten to fifteen years, nanobots will freeze your life at the age that you are and hold you there for fifteen or twenty years at the same level of vitality.[5] You're going to need a lot of money if you're going to keep up.

So the fallacy in the financial planning industry is that the decisions we're making today are based on the world being exactly the same twenty years from today. That's absolutely not the way it works.

That's why you need to think strategically. If you don't understand where your wealth is being eroded, then it's harder to accumulate wealth. And if you're not saving the right amount of money because your lifestyle's too high, you're going to reach a point of having to make major, major changes. Do you really want your future self to be pissed off at your current you? Do you really want to get to age seventy and have to tell your spouse, with whom you have always enjoyed a beautiful lifestyle, that you have to reduce your

---

5   Tom Koulopoulos, "The Most Dangerous and Disruptive Ideas According to Peter Diamandis and Ray Kurzweil," *Innovation Excellence*, accessed September 1, 2019, https://www.innovationexcellence.com/blog/2019/03/06/the-most-dangerous-and-disruptive-ideas-according-to-peter-diamandis-and-ray-kurzweil/.

spending by 80 percent because you don't have any money—because you already spent it all?

We all just live our lives. We run the kids to baseball, football, rugby, soccer, lacrosse, gymnastics, dance recitals. We shuffle them all over the place and spend money all the while. But we never really understand the impact of all that spending on our futures. We always just go through life thinking the future will be better. But you have to invest in the present. You have to understand the basics, or all the advanced planning won't matter.

If you want to improve your financial habits and your probability of success, ask yourself these questions:

- Do I want more money?

- Do I want less risk?

- Do I want to pay less in taxes?

- Do I want to pay less in fees?

- Do I want to have more benefits and more protection?

- Do I want to have more retirement income?

- Do I want to pass more to my family?

Or do you want the opposite of all these things? Most people have the opposite.

RATE OF RETURN—NO MAGIC FORMULA

Part of what I've been explaining circles back on the discussion from chapter one about rate of return. Rate of return is not the magic formula everyone would have you believe it is. It's simple math to see that the higher savings rate—20 percent versus 5 percent—will accumulate more money. Even if you have a linear plan that estimates a 10 percent return over a 5 percent return, then the person who is saving 10 percent is still going to accumulate more than the person saving 5 percent. Ask your child which is more: ten or five? Would they like ten M&M's candies or five? Even they know that the bigger the math, the bigger the gain.

As I mentioned before, everyone thinks that, in order to hit their goals, they've got to take on more risk. A 5 percent saver, in order to catch up with the big saver, is going to have to put their money in something that's going to make them a return along the lines of 10 percent or better. We're all trying to get the highest return on our money because the higher the return, the better off we're going to be—right? Well, that's not necessarily true. Taking more risk doesn't guarantee you more return. It can actually set you up to get dramatically hurt because, in order to get that rate of return, you may have to do things like allocating 100 percent of your money to the S&P 500. As we all know, that can be up one minute, down the next. And it's a little hard to stomach a 50 percent downturn.

Plus, there are varying tax rates to consider on those returns. A portfolio with stocks, bonds, and other investment vehicles in it is going to make returns from interest, dividends and qualified dividends, short-term and long-term realized capital gains, and unrealized capital gains—and all of those are taxed differently. For the sake of conversation, let's just assume that the return comes in thirds, taxed as follows (one-third each):

- Short-term gains as ordinary income

- Long-term capital gains at capital gain rate

- Unrealized gains, taxed in the future

Now, let's say that the 5 percent saver makes a 9.98 percent return, bringing them $2,824,000 worth of gains.

Instead of the portfolio being taxed all in one shot, only the short- and long-term gains would be taxed. If gains of $19,000 each resulted in $12,000 in taxes, that $12,000 is money that is not compounding, which can mean millions of dollars in lost capital. Instead of that $12,000 helping to earn $2,824,000, the portfolio ends up at $1,765,000. That's nearly $1 million of return lost from having to pay taxes. That's a huge opportunity cost in a portfolio.

> " YOUR FINANCIAL SUCCESS COMES MORE FROM YOUR SAVINGS RATE THAN FROM ANY RETURN ON YOUR MONEY.

After volatility, that portfolio could drop even more. For example, in 2008, the market ended down 37 percent. But it was down nearly 49 percent before the end of the year, and it came back up. Then in 2009, it was down another 25 percent, but ultimately ended with a 26 percent return. You had to experience that entire loss before you experienced the upswing. The bigger the downdraft, the more volatility-adjusted the return.

Rate of return is important, but it is not going to make or break a wealth plan. But savings rates will make all the difference. That's what I want you to understand more than anything else: *your financial success comes more from your savings rate than from any return on your money.*

And that savings rate has to be unbelievable. It has to be a habit. Charles Duhigg, author of *The Power of Habit: Why We Do What We Do in Life and Business*, wrote that the key to exercising regularly, losing weight, raising exceptional children, becoming more productive, building revolutionary companies and social movements, and achieving success is to understand how habits work.

The past has happened; you can't do anything about it now. It is what it is. But we need to unwind all the bad that's happened as much as possible, and then maximize all the good and keep maximizing it moving forward. The sooner we get control of your situation and help you develop good habits, the more money you're going to have in the future without having to take risk.

When we're doing your wealth planning, if I can help you drop a tax dollar, if I can find redundancies in a lifestyle or leaks in your plan—money that is being wasted without bringing enjoyment or benefits—then I can help you improve your savings rates and your probability of success in your financial life. It's that simple.

REMEMBER:

- Establishing your optimal savings rate is one of the most important parts of your financial plan.

- The higher your income level, the greater the percentage of your gross income that should go to savings.

- The goal is to put money into several different savings vehicles in order to create a constant inflow of money into savings.

- The Wealth Curve Blueprint looks at all of your income sources—including from rentals, investments, dividends, and bonuses—and determines your optimal savings rate.

- We help you identify places where you are spending money needlessly so that you can redirect that money to savings.

CHAPTER FOUR

RISK AND PROTECTION

Risk is not the fertilizer in your garden, it's the weeds.

—Ed Easterling

I've been talking about risk throughout the book, but what exactly is it? According to *Merriam-Webster*, risk is defined as: "possibility of loss or injury"; "someone or something that creates or suggests a hazard"; "the chance that an investment (such as a stock or commodity) will lose value."[6]

Basically, risk is something we all know as a situation involving exposure to danger. Where your financial plan is concerned, risk is not fertilizer that makes a portfolio magically grow.[7] But everyone

---

6   "Risk," *Merriam-Webster*, accessed May 30, 2019, https://www.merriam-web-ster.com/dictionary/risk.

7   As financial manager and researcher Ed Easterling alludes to in his book *Probable Outcomes: Secular Stock Market Insights* (Cypress House Press, 2011).

has their own definition of risk, depending on their own experiences.

In fact, on the subject of risk, the stock market is one of the first things that comes to mind for many people. And with that, they immediately think "big loss." But risk can be good or bad. Taking a big risk on something like the stock market and getting a hit can make you very successful—that's a good thing. Of course, exposing yourself to unnecessary dangers is when risk becomes a bad thing—whether in the stock market or elsewhere.

There are all kinds of risks when it comes to wealth. Understanding and controlling risk over extended periods of time is one of the most important aspects of the financial planning process. Here are some of the risks that can make a big impact on results.

Market risk is defined by the asset class that you are investing in.

Subsets of market risk include stock market risk. Investing in the US stock market usually involves the S&P 500, Nasdaq, or Dow Jones Industrial Average. Stock market risk also includes the broad markets and hedging out many stocks—in other words, owning several hundred stocks to balance out the ups and downs.

Another subset of market risk is industry risk, or putting all your money in one individual market sector. For instance, because people always need to power their homes and businesses, energy stocks might seem like a good sector to invest money in.

Then there is company risk, which is having your entire portfolio with a single company. People sometimes benefit from having single-stock concentration. There are a number of names on the *Forbes* 400 list whose wealth is in a single stock—Jeff Bezos of Amazon comes to mind. But sometimes having an entire portfolio made up of one stock is detrimental—like when a company goes under. There are many points in history where people had their entire life savings—their 401(k)s or pension plans—all in corporate stock and, when that company crashed, it destroyed the retirement plans of people who had spent their lives working for the company. Lucent Technologies and Enron are two examples.

Economic risks are all the types of monetary risks associated with a plan. These risks include factors such as income and liquidity, interest rate and taxes, withdrawal rates and estate taxes. Why are these considered to be risks? Let's look at the last in this list—estate tax.

In the past, there used to be high taxes imposed on an inheritance, but over time, the laws have changed. Currently, new tax laws have created complacency where estate taxes are concerned. As I write this book, anything below $11.4 million is exempt from federal inheritance tax, and many states have eliminated inheritance tax to compete with tax-free states that are drawing people in droves. At one point, anyone with wealth was moving south to avoid state-level inheritance tax. For a wealth plan with a nice $8 million estate through life insurance and investments, inheritance tax would not factor in. But in the future, the laws could change and create a completely different scenario—that's a risk. By taking action today in your plan through a coordinated use of wills, trusts, and beneficiary designations, we can eliminate the impact of inheritance taxes if the laws change again.

Another example is liquidity, which is one of the biggest risks that I see with a lot of businesses. Long-Term Capital, a massive hedge fund, demonstrates what can happen without liquidity. It represents one of the most epic failures of some of the smartest people on Wall Street. The company was borrowing money at a cheap rate and investing it in bonds at a long rate. It had $126 billion in assets and, at one point, was producing annual returns of more than 42 percent. Then everything went upside down. In 1998, it almost collapsed, which would have been the onset of a global financial crisis. The company had no liquidity, and it took a bailout by the Federal Reserve to save it and the financial markets as a whole.[8]

Assumption risks are based on current "knowns."

When building a wealth plan, we must make assumptions based on your "knowns"—you know you make a certain amount of money. You know you pay a certain level of tax. You know your family structure.

But too often, wealth plans are created based on the assumption that the variables in it are not going to change. In 1982, for instance, when a ten-year treasury was at 15.81 percent, $5 million in the bank at 15 percent created a lot of income.[9] But to base an entire wealth plan on the assumption that it will experience 15 percent growth for the long term would have created a lot of risk—as we all know, that kind of growth has not been consistent. In fact, my father, John P. Smallwood, has a saying:

> *Dying is bad enough, but dying in a down market really sucks.*

If you build a plan based on the assumption that you will live to age eighty-five, but you end up living a lot longer, that's assuming a level of risk. With that longer life comes the need for more income, more inflation hedges, more potential healthcare—just a whole series of "mores." And if you're out of money at age eighty-five, then anything beyond that is going to put tremendous pressure on family members to help you.

---

8   Kimberly Amadeo, "Long-Term Capital Management Hedge Fund Crisis," *The Balance*, January 25, 2019, accessed May 30, 2019, https://www.thebalance.com/long-term-capital-crisis-3306240.

9   Samantha M. Azzarello et al., "Guide to Markets: U.S. | Market Insights 1Q 2019 As of December 31, 2018," JP Morgan Asset Management, JPMorgan Chase & Co., 2019.

I felt that kind of pressure early in my career and early in my marriage. To help some in-laws with a financial problem, my wife and I bought their house and let them live there at a much-reduced rate. That expenditure, along with a monthly outlay of support money, put a tremendous amount of unplanned pressure on my plan. That was money that I wasn't able to reinvest back into my business or personal wealth plan, which created a long-term ripple effect. Every time you expose yourself to risk and you lose, the ripple effect of that loss is tremendous.

Poor assumptions often include the following:

- Your income is going to increase regularly and at a certain amount.

- You're going to save a certain amount of money every year.

- You're going to make a certain rate of return.

- Tax rates won't change.

- Dishwashers and refrigerators will never break down.

- You won't need new technology.

The truth is: everything in your plan will change from what it is today. Just like the boiling frog story from chapter one, everything is applying pressure to your plan and heading toward a boiling point.

Insurability risk is the ability to protect yourself against the risks in your plan. There are known risks, or things that you know may happen to you. And then there are unknown risks, or things you can't predict.

Your plan must include protections for a variety of known and unknown risks, including property and casualty, lawsuits, health, disability, long-term care, and death. The goal is to have maximum coverage for the least amount of cost so that, no matter the circumstance, your wealth is protected.

When creating a plan, people often don't want to calculate in risk because of the devastating picture it can paint. As human beings, we tend to underestimate the severity or consequences of risks until they impact us directly. That mindset, in itself, is risky when it comes to a wealth plan. When planning for the future, we must look at all the relationships that expose you to a level of potential danger. That's why we built the Wealth Curve Scorecard and use the Wealth Curve Simulation—to assess risks.

No one is immune to risk—now or in the future. The key when it comes to managing risk in financial planning is to figure what can be reduced or offloaded to a third party, an insurance company with strategies designed to protect you and your future.

When you're insuring something, you're technically covering it to replace its economic value in case of a loss. Economic value is "the value of an asset derived from its ability to generate income."[10] How much income can the asset produce? That's how economic value is determined. For example, if you buy a car for $50,000, what do you want to achieve by insuring it? If you were to get into an accident, you would want to be able to get a new car—especially if you just paid cash for that car. But you cannot insure something for greater than its economic value. You can't buy a $50,000 car and insure it for $200,000.

If you own something and a mishap occurs—it gets stolen or destroyed—you lose value unless you have it insured. Conversely, if you insure something and nothing happens to it during your entire lifetime, you lose money on the premiums that you paid in. Either way, you have a loss, and that loss also has an opportunity cost, meaning you lose any potential gain you could make on that dollar through an investment.

---

10   "Economic value," *InvestorWords*, accessed May 30, 2019, http://www.investor-words.com/1650/economic_value.html.

But here's a key point: Which loss is greater? The loss paid in premiums or the loss of the asset itself?

The goal with any insurance is to get the maximum protection with the least amount of cost. The idea is to take the risk and push it to the insurance company and protect your own money.

Let's look at it from the perspective of a home—a big asset for many people. If you own a house but don't insure it and it burns to the ground, you have a loss and are faced with rebuilding the house with your own funds. Once the house is rebuilt, you have value back, but you've given up the future wealth potential of the funds that were used to reconstruct the home. That would be devastating for most people.

> **THE GOAL WITH ANY INSURANCE IS TO GET THE MAXIMUM PROTECTION WITH THE LEAST AMOUNT OF COST. THE IDEA IS TO TAKE THE RISK AND PUSH IT TO THE INSURANCE COMPANY AND PROTECT YOUR OWN MONEY.**

As a simple, inexact example, let's say you have a $400,000 house on a lot worth $100,000, and you have $500,000 in cash in the bank. If the house is uninsured and burns to the ground, you will have to take $400,000 or so out of your cash to rebuild the house. Once it's built, the house will be worth $400,000, but at that point, your bank account will be down to $100,000. Altogether, then, your net wealth will be $600,000 ($500,000 house and land plus $100,000 cash), where only a few months prior it was $1 million.

If you had bought insurance for pennies on the dollar, the destroyed house could have been rebuilt, and you would also be able to keep your $400,000 in the bank. The insurance company would write a check for $400,000, which would keep your net wealth at $1 million.

Although the insurance policy does not add any value to your net wealth, its value is in the protection it provides.

If you owned a house for sixty years at $1,500 in annual premiums and never had a loss, that's $90,000 that you would never have the option of investing elsewhere for some sort of return. If that $1,500 per year were in the S&P, with a sixty-year average of over 9 percent, you could have $2.9 million by age eighty. You pay a premium for all those years and never benefit from it—which is really what we're hoping for. But your success in never having to make a claim means losing the opportunity to invest that money and make money from it. Think the house will appreciate that much? Now think about that in terms of your car insurance—over the same time period, you're losing even more opportunity.

That's why it's so important to ensure you're getting the maximum protection with the least amount of cost. The whole idea is to take the risk and push it to the insurance company and protect your own money.

Homeowners' policies also typically include liability coverage to protect you from lawsuits. That coverage protects the money you have in the bank. If someone comes on your property and gets bitten by your pit bull, they'll likely sue you. (I have bichon shih tzus—they're benign, although one of them thinks she's a pit bull. Vicious little mothers—I'm joking, of course.) The point being, without liability coverage, you'll have to write the check for your dog biting that person on your property. No one wants that to happen, because those checks can mean a lifetime of liens for someone just entering the workforce, and they can decimate accumulated wealth for someone ready to retire.

One of the most basic financial strategies for reducing risk and protecting the assets you have accumulated is to have adequate insurance for the unknowns in life. Yet too many people lack these protections.

PROTECTING YOUR MOST VALUABLE ASSET

Like your other assets, you have an economic value—it's your ability to earn income. It's simply a measure of your current income production and the length of time you will produce that income. It does not capture any earning potential above your present level. But, although your ability to earn income is your most valuable asset, it's often your most underinsured asset.

What would happen if your ability to get up every morning and earn an income were impacted by a long-term disability event? What would that do to your wealth potential? Without proper protection, you will not be able to accumulate the amount of wealth that you want, retire when you want to, or have the kind of retirement that you envision.

Yet the impact of a long-term disability on a wealth plan is often overlooked, and those who do have coverage typically don't know how much they have. I was working with a client recently who thought they had $10,000 per month of disability coverage. But we when checked, we found out they only had $4,000. According to the Council for Disability Awareness, the odds of a worker entering the workforce today becoming disabled before they retire are about 25 percent. Yet, fewer than half of American adults (48 percent) have enough savings to cover even three months of expenses should they become unable to work.[11]

When it comes to disability insurance, there are four potential outcomes:

1. If you don't own the coverage and nothing happens, you win. You live out your life with no disability and are able to

---

11   "Chances of Disability," *Council for Disability Awareness*, March 28, 2018, accessed May 30, 2019, https://disabilitycanhappen.org/disability-statistic/.

continue working and saving money toward the future.

2. If you become disabled without coverage, then running out of money is more likely a matter of *when*, not *if.*

3. If you become disabled and you own the proper amount of disability coverage, your wealth plan can continue as if you were able to go on working.

4. If you own the coverage and you don't become disabled, you'll be glad you're protected, but you'll feel as if you wasted money and have lost wealth potential from the premiums paid in.

Here's why disability is such an important part of a financial plan. Let's use one of the households from the last chapter as an example. The wage earner is forty-five years old and earns an annual income of $250,000. The household lifestyle costs are $151,000 annually. Accumulated wealth is a combination of assets worth approximately $500,000. Annual savings are $50,000.

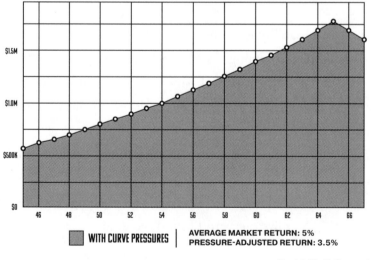

AVERAGE MARKET RETURN: 5%
PRESSURE-ADJUSTED RETURN: 3.5%

WITH CURVE PRESSURES

Fig. 4.1: Wealth Curve potential.

The Wealth Curve potential for this supersaver household at age sixty-five (retirement) is approximately $1,756,000 after curve pressures.

But what would this plan look like if the wage earner became disabled at age forty-eight and had no disability insurance?

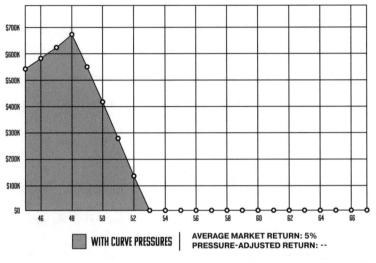

Fig. 4.2: Wealth Curve potential with a disability.

By this model, just five years from becoming disabled, the account value is at zero. Now what? The result could mean losing the house, no college for the kids, maybe even moving in with family.

What would happen if the wage earner had purchased the proper amount of disability insurance for their unique situation?

Let's assume that we find the money in their financial strategy to pay for the disability coverage, and they don't work for a company that provides it, or they decide not to maximize the corporate benefit because of the parameters of the contract. That leaves them with buying the insurance on their own at $3,000 per year. Instead of saving $50,000 a year, they'll now be saving $47,000. But with the disability insurance, if something happens, their benefit is $11,000 a month, payable to age seventy, with a cost-of-living rider that ranges somewhere between 2 percent and 6 percent.

Without disability insurance, this household was on track to accumulate $1,756,000, compared to $1,653,000 after the cost of owning disability coverage. That's a $103,000 difference in twenty years, which is equivalent to $39,000 as I write this book, based on a net return of 5 percent over the time frame.

A multiphase disability strategy creates layers of protection that go beyond lifestyle expenses; it looks for ways to continue the savings element of a long-term financial strategy. Here's what the plan could look like if the wage earner becomes disabled and has the proper amount of coverage.

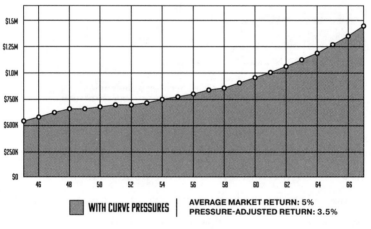

WITH CURVE PRESSURES | AVERAGE MARKET RETURN: 5%
PRESSURE-ADJUSTED RETURN: 3.5%

Fig. 4.3: Wealth Curve potential with a disability and coverage.

This simulation shows that the account would allow the household to sustain its lifestyle beyond the wage earner reaching age sixty-seven.

There are also catastrophic riders available that can pay an additional monthly benefit for a disability that leaves the insured unable to satisfy two of the six acts of daily living—eating, bathing, dressing, grooming, having mobility, and toileting. Should that kind of disability occur, here's what the plan could look like. This strategy provides a $10,000 per month benefit and assumes a 2 percent inflation rate

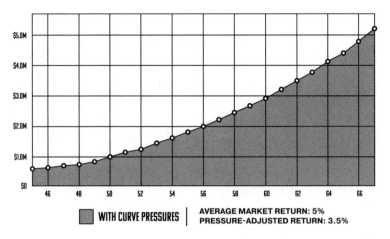

WITH CURVE PRESSURES | AVERAGE MARKET RETURN: 5%
PRESSURE-ADJUSTED RETURN: 3.5%

Fig. 4.3: Wealth Curve potential with a disability and coverage.

on that benefit.

With this simulation, the account actually surpasses the initial $1,756,000 wealth potential with an account value of $4,425,000 at retirement.

Given the impact long-term disability can have on your Wealth Curve, doesn't the protection seem worth it? Look at it this way. You have two compensation packages: one is a job where you make $250,000 per year, and if you become disabled, you get zero. The other is a job where you make $246,000 per year, and if you become disabled, you get $11,000 a month tax-free. Which job are you taking?

When you build a financial strategy, you know that tax rates will change, interest rates will change, markets will have risk, and you may have a long-term disability event. Protecting yourself properly will not prevent you from having wealth; it can actually help you create more wealth during your lifetime. It will help you be better prepared for all the disasters that could or could not happen to you. With this discussion, I'm not trying to scare the living crap out of you. I just don't want to be the advisor if you do have an event and are not covered. Not on my watch.

Determining the proper amount of disability insurance is a matter of figuring out how much protection you need should the worst happen. Then, we must look at your plan and find the waste— money just being sucked away by lifestyle, taxes, and other factors— to see if we can free up money out of those areas for the coverage. If you can figure out how to recapture money that's being pissed away (my technical term for waste in a plan) and push it to something better, like protecting yourself, wouldn't it be worth it to reduce your exposure to risk?

We can help you devise strategies to reposition money so that you have maximum protection throughout your entire lifetime with the least amount of cost, allowing you to spend the maximum amount of wealth and pass the maximum amount of wealth to your family. Because insurance is designed to protect the economic value of you, the individual. It protects your ability to earn money and accumulate wealth without being encumbered by financial pressure. By having an insurance company take on a portion of the risk of replacing a house or car, of getting sued, of becoming disabled or needing long-term care, you can be prepared to defend yourself and protect your assets beyond your current resources.

REMEMBER:

- You have risk, and it's everywhere.

- The risks that are in your plan are unique to you.

- You're probably not insured properly or protected properly.

- The Wealth Curve Scorecard can help measure where you're deficient in known risks.

- A Wealth Curve Simulation can look at potential known risks and then try to think about what could happen.

CHAPTER FIVE

TAXES AND FEES– THE GREAT WEALTH DESTRUCTORS

Two of the greatest disruptors of wealth and its potential are taxation and fees. Income taxes, payroll taxes, sales taxes, state-level taxes— there are myriad ways your money is taxed. Fees are incurred when implementing a financial plan and purchasing financial products— they are embedded in every product out there. It doesn't matter as much what the taxes or fees are; what matters is understanding the effect they are having on your wealth.

Nobody likes to pay taxes. Nobody likes to pay fees. I hate paying taxes and fees.

When it comes to taxes and fees, most financial strategies are missing the fundamentals, leaving you to pay much more than you should over your lifetime. A lot of investments are driven based upon some sort of tax or fee savings. Maybe you've seen the ads out there trying to get everybody into a tax-free or low-fee retirement plan? Well, they may have tax-free or low-fee components, but they're rather extreme and very risky. For example, a quick tax law change, and the entire strategy can be gone—poof, just like that.

Everybody reading this right now has a slightly different mix of income sources, and those dictate and modify how you're being taxed and the fees you are paying. Because of that, the strategy for you is not the strategy for your brother, your neighbor, your best friend. Your dynamics are different.

But there are some fundamental concepts of taxes and fees that apply to the financial planning process. The goal is for you to have multiple sources of retirement income that balance out taxes and fees. That way, if one or more of the sources dries up, or if tax law changes a source or two, then the impact on your portfolio will be minimal.

To keep your retirement plan from going up in smoke, we want to build you a rock-solid retirement plan that generates income from predictable and reliable sources that maximize a number of benefits. The sources of income, and some tax implications, include the following:

Social Security. You and your employer pay a lot of money in every year. In 2019, the maximum Social Security tax was 7.65 percent of $132,900. There's a lot of talk about when to take Social Security, with pros and cons for and against deferring. There's no one-size-fits-all solution. What's important is to understand what's right for you.

Pensions. If you have a pension, you have several options for when to begin taking the income. Most pension incomes are life-only mode. If you die before taking the pension, your survivors may receive no benefit, or that benefit may have certain limits. Some pensions offer a joint and survivor option, where the benefits are reduced during your lifetime and then a predetermined percentage passes to your survivor. The key is to understand your pension benefits and ways to maximize them.

Interest. Bank accounts, bonds, and savings accounts generate interest. These interest rates may be low, but they are less volatile than some other sources.

Ordinary dividends. These ensure you generate income through dividends from stocks and bonds.

Qualified dividends. These get a preferred tax treatment. Instead of being taxed as ordinary income, they are taxed at the capital gains rate.

Tax-free dividends. Tax-free dividends come from municipal bonds and other related assets.

Whole life insurance dividends. These are tax-free until you reach the basis of what you paid into the contract. They offer guaranteed increases and are a good retirement income source.

Capital gains income. This is taxed at a different rate than ordinary income, and you're realizing the gains on your portfolio over a specific time frame. This is another great source of retirement income.

Business income. A great part of any retirement plan is owning a business and having a management team or family member run it. However, the goal while working in the business is to take as much money out of the business as possible, protect it, and grow it, so that if the company doesn't sell, then it doesn't affect retirement income. If the company ultimately sells, it's just gravy.

Royalties. This income comes from different types of investments or inventions, or from authoring a book or piece of artwork (copyright). It may not apply to you (yet), but it's a good source of retirement income with unique tax benefits.

Partnership income. Income from partnerships includes investing in different types of entities. This type of income could be tax advantaged because it's sheltered by depreciation.

Real estate rental. Second homes, an apartment, a commercial property, or an office building can bring additional income and be highly valuable assets.

Reverse mortgage. A reverse mortgage could generate a consistent tax-free cash flow. Usually, you cannot outlive it because they are nonrecourse loans. That means the house is the only form of security.

Immediate annuity income. This is, in essence, your own private pension. You give money to an insurance company and, in return, it guarantees a lifetime of income for you, your spouse, or both. This can come with unique tax benefits—for example, the exclusion ratio, which is the portion of your return that is not subject to taxes. Let's say you receive a significant monthly payment. One portion is a return on the principal, and the other is interest. You only pay tax on the interest portion.

Annuity income. These can be either fixed or variable. Annual income is taken from the annuity. Depending upon your basis in the contract (IRA or non-IRA), it could have unique tax benefits. It may also provide lifetime income guarantees on the sections.

Roth income. Roth income could be tax-free in retirement. It currently is.

IRA income. The plan with an IRA is to defer taxes to a lower bracket when you are in retirement.

Principal paydowns. Done strategically, this concept can provide critical income during different phases of retirement. Think of it as the bucket strategy: one bucket for the first ten to fifteen years of retirement, then the next, then the next. A principal paydown can provide unique tax benefits as you spread out tax liability over a multiyear time frame.

With all of these in place, you can expect rising income, protection, backups, redundancies, and inflation hedges.

Plus, all of these sources of retirement income hit your tax return differently and create fees differently, and there are nuances to each of them. Notice that "work" is not on this list—this strategy is designed to cover your core expenses for food, entertainment, real estate, and other basics of daily life without you having to work anymore.

Taxes and fees are complex subjects, but there are some fundamentals you should know when planning for retirement.

Let's look at some tax strategies and how they play into your plan to see whether they are working for you.

MARGINAL AND EFFECTIVE TAX RATES

One of the fundamentals to understand is the difference between marginal and effective tax rates. Essentially, the marginal tax bracket is the tax paid on the last dollars of income, and the effective bracket is how much tax you paid overall divided by your income.

Take, for instance, married filing jointly on a current tax sheet. Currently, there are seven tax brackets—these are considered marginal tax brackets. Bonus income, interest income, dividend income, and so on are taxed in the marginal bracket. A deduction such as mortgage interest or from a 401(k) also occurs in the marginal tax bracket.

In 2019, if your income was over $612,350, the last dollars were taxed at 37 percent. But the money from zero to $19,400 was taxed at 10 percent, from $19,400 to $78,950 at 12 percent, and so on. Again, these are marginal taxes.

The effective tax bracket is, in essence, where income falls in this and the average amount of tax paid across all of those tax brackets. If you make $100,000 and pay $15,000 in federal income tax, your effective bracket is 15 percent. But if you make that $100,000 in the marginal tax bracket from $78,951 to $168,000, all those last dollars are taxed at 22 percent.

If you understand both of these numbers, you can begin to understand how to reduce the taxation of your income down into another bracket so that it's occurring at the marginal bracket, not at your effective bracket.

Let me take a minute to share with you a little history on the tax code, which might provide a little more insight into marginal versus effective tax rates and the impact they have had over time.

Income taxes have historically been very high, and payroll taxes have been increasing over time. What's been declining is corporate income tax. How does that affect your financial plan? Well, income and payroll taxes directly impact your financial strategy. But let's take a quick look back to see where we were, and where we are today.

President Abraham Lincoln enacted the first income tax in 1861 to help pay for the Civil War. The tax was 3 percent on income over $800. Then, in 1913, the Sixteenth Amendment gave Congress the power to tax all forms of income. At that time, a 7 percent tax was placed on income.

Since then, there has been a marginal bracket. By 1918, tax for the highest earners was at 78 percent. In 1927, it dropped to 25 percent; then in 1946, it went roaring up to 94 percent—the last tax dollars, that marginal bracket, were taxed at 94 percent. Future president Ronald Reagan wrote a book in which he stated that, during this time period, he made $1 million, but because he didn't have any tax planning, he paid close to $900,000 in income tax. That seems almost unfathomable, but that was the reality back then. And that kind of income tax went on for nearly twenty years.

After that, the taxes began to drop, down to around 70 percent, then around 50 percent, and then, during the Reagan era, to about 28 percent. Since then, the taxes have been slowly creeping back up. I've included a more detailed history of the tax brackets in appendix A. In it, you can see that back in 1913, there were seven tax brackets, from the first bracket of 1 percent to the top bracket of 7 percent. The top income bracket was over $500,000—adjusted for inflation to 2014, that would be close to $12 million of income taxed at 7 percent. But only three years later, the top bracket rate was at 67 percent, jumping from $500,000 to $2 million, or more than $36 million in 2014 dollars.

At the same time all this is happening, there are other taxes putting pressure on your financial strategy. For instance, dividends, interest, and capital gains are considered to be earned income—money that is subject to tax. And while you might be able to take advantage of itemized deductions on your tax return, deductions are always changing—since the 1980s and 1990s, many of them have been lowering or are being phased out.

> THE POINT IS THAT TAX BRACKETS AND TAX RATES ARE MOVING TARGETS. WHAT MAY BENEFIT YOU TODAY MAY ACTUALLY MEAN ADDITIONAL TAXES NEXT YEAR OR TEN YEARS FROM NOW.

The point is that tax brackets and tax rates are moving targets. What may benefit you today may actually mean additional taxes next year or ten years from now.

How does all of this affect financial planning strategy? One area where this becomes crucially important is with strategies involving tax deferral.

THE TAX DEFERRAL DEBATE

Tax deferral strategies are intended to defer paying taxes on certain assets based on the concept of moving from a higher tax bracket to a lower tax bracket at some date in the future. So instead of paying taxes on $10,000 today, when you are in a higher tax bracket, you will pay taxes on that $10,000 later when you are in retirement and reporting in a lower tax bracket. That's the idea anyway, but there is much debate in the industry about whether it's a good idea to defer taxes until a future date. Deferring, some argue, allows you to have the money to spend today to invest in other vehicles. But if you defer and don't end up in a lower tax bracket, what do you really gain? The debate has gone on for years and shows no signs of stopping.

The tax rate is not always in our favor. Tax rates and tax brackets have changed over time, sometimes going up and sometimes going down. If you defer to a future date and the rates are at a place where they are beneficial, then it's a win. But if you are in a higher tax rate in the future, you can lose. You might even end up paying more than if you had not deferred.

Maybe the best demonstration of where this comes into play is with traditional IRAs or 401(k)s and Roth IRAs or 401(k)s. The major difference between traditional versus Roth is that traditional is a pretax investment while the Roth is post-tax. As a pretax investment, if you're making $100,000 and you put $10,000 into a traditional IRA or 401(k), then you're going to pay tax on $90,000—but you're deferring your tax payments on the $10,000 until some date in the future. With the Roth IRA or Roth 401(k), both of which are post-tax, taxes are paid on the money first, and then they are not paid again until later when the money is withdrawn. There are limits to your contribution levels and other rules that I'm not including here.

If we had a magical crystal ball, we might be able to see whether you will be in a higher or lower tax bracket twenty years from now. There is no telling what the tax rates will be at that time. Looking at the history of the marginal tax brackets, as I write this book, we are in one of the lowest points ever.

Let's look at some potential scenarios to demonstrate how this all works.

Assume you're in a 30 percent tax bracket. Without putting $10,000 into a plan, then $3,000 in tax must be paid on that $10,000, leaving you with $7,000. On the other hand, if $10,000 is put into a plan, then it's working for you for the next twenty years or so. While it's in the plan, the taxes are deferred. If the money has a 6 percent rate of return, just that one deposit with no matching contribution could grow to $32,000. If you're in the same tax bracket after twenty years, then 30 percent of that $32,000, or $9,600, goes to the IRS. That means you have $22,400. The question is: Did you make any money?

The government is investing with you on a side-by-side basis; if you give the government $3,000, and it makes 6 percent on that money over twenty years, that's $9,621.

The takeaway here is that if you end up in a 20 percent tax bracket when it's time to withdraw the money, then you have a windfall, regardless of your rate of return. But do you have control over the brackets of the future? And do you know for certain what your level of income will be at that time?

Although there is a valid perception by many people that they will be in a lower tax bracket when they retire, the truth is that most of our clients aren't. The house is paid for, the kids are out of the house, they lose deductions, and they end up in a higher tax bracket. There are financial strategies that can help mitigate taxation so that deferral is part of a plan, but not all of it.

I want you to know where you are in your bracket. I want you to understand where your assets are. And then based on that information, determine whether deferral is something that makes sense for your plan. Instead of just automatically looking at deferral as a tax strategy, what's a more appropriate and effective strategy?

QUALIFIED PLANS—OTHER PITFALLS

Historically, qualified plans such as 401(k)s, IRAs, and Roth accounts have been under attack. For instance, in the mid-1990s, there was an excise tax. If you had accumulated over $750,000 in a qualified retirement plan and you died, the amount over $750,000 would be subject to a 15 percent excise tax in addition to the regular income tax.

There are other factors to consider with qualified plans.

Withdrawal rules. There are specific rules—and potential penalties—for withdrawing from accounts. Withdrawing before age fifty-nine-and-a-half brings a 10 percent penalty. Then, at seventy-and-a-half, there are required minimum distributions (RMDs). With RMDs, there is a 50 percent penalty for not withdrawing the right about of money. For example, if the RMD calculation is $10,000 and you don't withdraw that, then you'll pay a $5,000 penalty. Plus, depending on the account, you have to pay taxes according to your bracket.

Those RMDs, when combined with other income, might

actually push you into a higher tax bracket where all income is hit with a higher tax rate. That can happen year after year.

A common trap that I often see is a person who retires early and then spends the next ten years living only on their aftertax money. They don't withdraw from a pension or an IRA or start taking Social Security. They're in a lower tax bracket, and they're not taking money from other sources. Then they reach age seventy-and-a-half, and they're subject to RMDs. Now they're in a higher tax bracket, and all they've got left are qualified plans, but they've missed the window of taking money out during this lower tax period, and they're subject to the government changing the taxes.

If you retire and all of your money is in retirement plans, you're subject to whatever the tax rates are at that moment. If you have $1 million accumulated in a qualified retirement plan, and you need to pull out $40,000 on a 4 percent withdrawal rate, you're in a 20 percent effective tax rate as the brackets currently stand. You will pay $8,000 in tax. Now your $40,000 becomes $32,000 after tax. But what if the IRS changes the brackets and you end up with a 30 percent tax? Now, you've got $12,000 on that $40,000, leaving you with $28,000. That's a 66 percent increase in taxes, going from 20 to 30 percent. What are your choices then? You'll either have to reduce your lifestyle or take more money out of your qualified plan to net the $32,000 you were trying to get.

The forces of taxes can accelerate your spend down—do you have enough to keep from running out of money?

If you're retired and don't have income sources, start pulling money out of those qualified plans as soon as possible. If you've accumulated too much money in a qualified retirement plan and you don't have enough money out, you might want to take it out early prior to age fifty-nine-and-a-half using one of the tax codes to avoid the 10 percent penalty.

Lack of liquidity. One of the issues with qualified plans is their lack of liquidity. In the accumulation phase, qualified plans can lock up money you need. There are certain rules that allow for some withdrawals to be made in specific circumstances, but for the most part, once the money is in the plan, it's there to stay until retirement.

The other problem when it comes to liquidity and qualified plans sometimes happens to those retirees that I mentioned in the last example. They're spending all their non-IRA assets early in retirement and slowly eroding their liquid cash. What sometimes happens is that they need liquidity; they need money to pay for a child's wedding or to help fund a grandchild's college education. Without cash or liquid reserves, they have to either borrow money or take a large distribution from an IRA account. Because of the impact of taxes, they might have to withdraw significantly more in order to have the net they need for the gift.

Compound taxes. Tax strategy in the accumulation phase is one of the most important parts of a wealth plan. A forty-five-year-old with a savings rate of 6 percent putting away $51,000 per year could accumulate a healthy balance of $2.5 million by age sixty-five. That's the miracle of compound savings.

But that doesn't take into account the miracle of compound taxation. Early on in my career, Castiglione, creator of the Leap System, explained the concept of compound taxation. It's something that you know is occurring in your plan but can't quite put your finger on.

Basically, with compound taxation, money is eroding all the time. Each year that an account grows, the investor's tax liability grows along with it. Interest earnings, along with dividends and capital gains, get larger over time as the investment gains in value. If you make $30,000 in interest, dividends, or capital gains, taxes must be paid on that money.

If the gains the first year include $30,000 worth of interest but at the 30 percent tax bracket, then you'll have to pay $9,000 more in taxes. So now, instead of having $51,000 to invest, you only have $42,000. What do you think that will do to your compounding potential? It's going to kill it.

Taxes must be paid from your earnings or from your account. But however they're paid, they are destroying your wealth potential. In this account, instead of having $2,523,000, there is only $1,859,000. That's a loss of $674,000. That's compound taxation.

Compound fees. Just as compound taxation is destroying your financial plan, so are compound fees. Fees can vary widely and may include commissions, transaction or trading costs, optional riders, and more. The best way to deal with fees is to first identify them and then look for ways to minimize them without significantly altering the products in your portfolio. The goal is to maximize the products while minimizing fees.

Compound taxation and compound fees can destroy your wealth. Taxes and fees have been problems forever, but we blindly go down these roads where we have no control over them. Your strategy should be more than just compounding blindly into the future.

Qualified plans can be among the most powerful assets that you have. I'm not saying that qualified plans are crap and that you should get out of them. I'm saying you should really think about them and

> TAXES AND FEES HAVE BEEN PROBLEMS FOREVER, BUT WE BLINDLY GO DOWN THESE ROADS WHERE WE HAVE NO CONTROL OVER THEM. YOUR STRATEGY SHOULD BE MORE THAN JUST COMPOUNDING BLINDLY INTO THE FUTURE.

understand their power.

The key thing to understand is that having all your money in one type of thing gives you no control over your money and how it's going to be taxed or the fees that will be charged. Every dollar that went into certain qualified plans will have fees on the way in and along the way, and it will be taxed on the way out.

SYSTEMATIC WITHDRAWALS

Systematic withdrawals, if done properly, can significantly reduce the tax impact on an investment portfolio. Let's say, late in 1989, you placed a lump sum of $100,000 in an S&P 500 index fund with a good, long track record. Instead of leaving the funds in the account, however, and relying solely on compound interest, you took $6,000 from the account each year and repositioned those assets elsewhere. After twenty years, the fund balance would have reached $243,191— an annual gain of 7.92 percent that exceeds the return earned by leaving the funds in the account. Why? Because taking those withdrawals undercuts the impact of compounded taxes. Over time, the tax obligation would be $30,451, or $13,622 less than leaving the money in the account.

In addition, the other $6,000 per year could be invested in something like a conservative, low-risk, tax-free bond fund. Even if the fund returned only 3.37 percent annually during the twenty-year period, it would still add up to $201,426. Bond funds are subject to credit risk, interest rate risk, and prepayment risk, as disclosed in each bond's prospectus.

THE BEST TOOL? GOOD PLANNING

There are a lot of different opinions in the financial planning industry—if you do a 401(k), you're a moron; if you don't do a 401(k), you're a moron. But the truth is that it's not black and white. All of these are just financial tools, and as we all know, we only use the tool if it's appropriate for the job.

Good planning gives you options. That includes having income from all the sources mentioned at the beginning of the chapter. And it includes having multiple strategies to offset the taxation on qualified money coming out. Some of those strategies include the following:

- Charitable remainder trusts

- Rental properties and mortgages

- 529 plans

- Annuities

- Nonqualified assets

- Life insurance

- Tax-free municipal bonds

Before making another contribution to a qualified plan, understand marginal and effective tax brackets and fees. If you're in low marginal and effective tax brackets, Roth contributions may make a tremendous amount of sense. For a twenty-five-year-old in a low tax bracket—hopefully the lowest of their working life—a Roth deferral probably makes sense. If all your money is in qualified plans and there is nothing in nonqualified plans or other assets, it might be a good idea to back off.

If you are self-employed and don't have a lot of employees, putting together a qualified plan might make sense for asset protection. But if you have a lot of employees whom you have to put money in for, it may not be the best choice. I encounter business owners frequently who are sponsoring some sort of retirement plan for their employees. They think it's for them. But it's really for their employees. Let's say the employer is putting $80,000 into the plan—$50,000 for themselves and $30,000 for employees. But if the employer pays, let's say, 30 percent tax on that $50,000, they only have $32,000 left. Employees get $30,000, and the employer ends up with $32,000, whereas if the employer were to pay 30 percent tax on the $80,000 and not do a qualified plan, then they would have $56,000. A qualified plan is a good retention tool, but too often small employers just implement them without really knowing what they're doing to their own plan.

Tax planning should not happen in March, just prior to filing a tax return. And fees should be understood before going into an investment. Organizing income sources so that they hit your tax return the right way and incur the lowest fees should be a deliberate strategy that is taken on every single quarter, every single year.

By doing a Wealth Curve Blueprint, we're going to figure out your income sources and marginal and effective tax brackets and any fees associated with the components of your plan, and then we're going to work toward repositioning your money to reduce fees and costs, increase your savings rate, increase your retirement income, and put more benefits and protection around your wealth.

REMEMBER:

- Taxes and fees are going to erode your wealth.

- If you don't understand marginal and effective tax, you could end up exposing your money to more and more drain.

- If you don't understand the fees associated with your plan, you could end up exposing your money to more and more drain.

- Where are your income sources? Where are they showing on your tax return?

- What can you do now to maintain growth potential but be much more tax and fee efficient?

- Understand, based upon where you are today, where you will end up in fifteen or twenty years if you change nothing.

CHAPTER SIX

A BEAUTIFUL BALANCE

In chapter four, I talked about insuring yourself against risk, including the risk of losing your most valuable asset—your ability to work.

Every type of insurance you own is designed to protect you in hopes that the event being insured never happens—except for life insurance. Life insurance is the only definitive outcome. The question is, will you be insured upon your death?

The goal with insurance is to have the maximum amount of coverage during your entire life owned in the most efficient manner so that your wealth and its potential are achieved, enjoyed, and passed on to your heirs. You don't want to be overprotected and not have any money going into savings.

In short, you must have what I like to call a "beautiful balance."

Unfortunately, what often happens is that people pay for a life insurance policy during their accumulation years, and then when they retire, they lose the policy because of a change in premiums. If you lose your life insurance in retirement, then you're following the masses and losing millions of dollars in potential for your family. Remember: The purpose of a great financial strategy is to reduce taxes, risk, and fees and costs while increasing your savings rate and retirement income, putting more benefits and protection around your wealth, and passing more money on to the family. Losing your life insurance in retirement defeats that whole strategy.

Just like other types of coverage, life insurance is designed to protect economic value—your economic value. That is based on multiple factors, including your current assets, or how much you have accumulated, and your earnings, or how much you make each year.

Life insurance companies have a formula to determine the maximum amount of insurance they will issue on an individual. The formulas range by age and from company to company but are generally a multiple of earned income and current level of assets. For instance, a thirty-year-old individual making $100,000 per year might be able to obtain about twenty-five times that amount, or $2.5 million in coverage, plus assets. A seventy-year-old retiree with a net worth of $1 million may only be able to acquire that same amount in life insurance, or one multiplied by net worth. The closer an individual gets to retirement, the lower the multiple of coverage. By the way, that calculation is how life insurance companies determine another person's economic value as well. If, for instance, you get in a car accident with another vehicle that is your fault, someone in the other car is killed, and you are sued as a result, then the insurers look at that person's economic value. If he was age fifty and made $200,000 a year, then his economic value is determined to be twenty times that, or $4 million. Do you have enough liability coverage to protect yourself against that kind of lawsuit?

LIFE INSURANCE—SO MISUNDERSTOOD

Insuring your life should take into account your economic value because your ability to earn and accumulate income are your greatest assets, and your death is an economic loss for your family or those who count on you. Yet life insurance is a category of wealth planning where people make some of the worst decisions. For many people, the discussion of life insurance is one that comes with much misunderstanding and bad information. The space is filled with many different companies, many different types of products, and many different opinions as to what is best. It's very common to hear that you don't need life insurance in retirement at all. Does that really seem logical?

Think about it: Are you more likely to die at age forty-five or age eighty-five? Before retirement or after? If you die in retirement, what are the risks?

- **Social Security.** The first risk is that your spouse will lose your Social Security. When one spouse dies, one of the checks goes away. That's a dramatic reduction in most people's income.

- **Pension.** When a person dies, their pension gets dramatically reduced or eliminated for their spouse.

- **Taxes.** Tax filings upon the death of a spouse go from married filing jointly to single—placing the survivor in a higher tax bracket.

- **Debts.** Uninsured medical expenses, long-term care, and round-the-clock nursing homes can burn up a lot of cash. Business debts can also leave an estate with a lot of creditors in hot pursuit.

- **Lawsuits.** Settlements from lawsuits can draw from an estate even after death.

Again, you are the most important part of your plan as the person earning the wealth. Seeing all that can happen before or during retirement, why wouldn't someone want life insurance throughout their life?

The cost of owning the proper amount of life insurance and type today should not negatively impact your future wealth potential and your retirement income. Money saved on taxes, fees, expenses, and in other areas of the plan can be used to reduce the impact of owning the proper amount of coverage on your wealth plan. Properly done, the coverage should even help to increase both your wealth potential and retirement income.

When conducting a life insurance simulation, we determine what would happen if death were to occur yesterday. Consider, for instance, an example where a forty-five-year-old who makes $250,000 a year died without having life insurance. In this simulation, the family's lifestyle would be reduced to $21,520.

But if that same forty-five-year-old had obtained the maximum coverage of around $5 million for an annual premium of $4,000, that would bring $250,000 a year of pretax income after death.

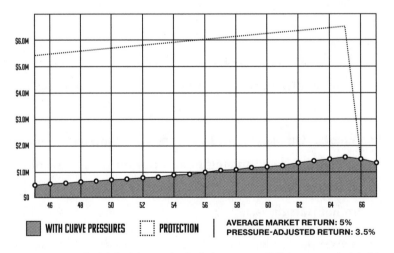

WITH CURVE PRESSURES   PROTECTION | **AVERAGE MARKET RETURN: 5%**
PRESSURE-ADJUSTED RETURN: 3.5%

Fig. 6.1: Family income after death of wage earner with life insurance and net death benefit.

In fact, the wealth plan could even be on track to accumulate $1,532,000, with a net death benefit of over $5 million.

In fact, if this forty-five-year-old individual died two years after purchasing a policy, at age forty-seven, his or her family would be able to maintain their standard of living and have increasing assets that, by age sixty-five, could be over $6,399,000.

Again, life insurance attempts to protect against the loss of your present economic value. Put it in terms of real estate: If you owned a rental property that produced $250,000 per year, how much would you insure it for? If you insure it for just $250,000, that will not provide enough capital to replace the cash flow lost. If the building burned to the ground, how much money would be needed to rebuild the structure? Assuming a simplistic return of 4 percent, the building is worth $6,250,000. That represents the amount of coverage it should have.

UNDERSTANDING TERM VERSUS WHOLE LIFE

There are basically three types of life insurance: term, whole, and universal. Term is essentially what I call a "rental" type of life insurance—people often buy the policy for most of their life, but then drop it in retirement. Whole is in place for your entire life—it has guaranteed premiums, cash values, and death benefits, and it has the potential to earn greater than the guarantees based on the performance of the issuing insurance company. Universal is basically a hybrid between term and whole life.

With a term life insurance policy, typically the individual pays a level premium for several years before it increases a considerable amount. For example, the guaranteed annual premium may range from $645 to $1,315 and then increase to $10,285 ten years after the individual purchases the policy.

You can buy ten-, fifteen-, twenty-, and thirty-year level term policies. They all work exactly the same way—they offer a level premium for a set period of time, and then that premium increases significantly. If you are insurable at the point that the term life premiums increase, then you may be able to buy new coverage. If you are not insurable at that point, then to keep your policy, you'll have to continue to pay the premium: maybe $10,285 at age fifty-six, $11,005 at age fifty-seven, and so on. Every year that you get older, the policy appears to be getting more and more expensive. In reality, it's just the way that term policies are designed—the mortality cost is amortized at the end of the policy instead of over the life of the policy.

But that increase in premium is why many people drop term life when they reach the point in life when it's needed most. They pay for it for twenty or thirty years, and then come retirement age, they can no longer afford the premiums. How would you like to have that conversation with your wife? "Honey, I'm so happy we've been married for so long; it's been a wonderful life and I really love you. But now I'm going to drop my million dollars' worth of life insurance because I can no longer pay for it—happy anniversary."

> "YOU ALSO LOSE ALL THE PREMIUM MONEYS THAT YOU PAID IN, AND YOU LOSE THE OPPORTUNITY COSTS OF THOSE PREMIUMS. AND THAT IS ETERNAL WEALTH THROUGH MULTIPLE GENERATIONS LOST FOREVER.

It's unbelievable. After twenty years of paying premiums, you might spring for one more year in hopes that you die and your family receives your benefit. But then you don't die, so you pay another, higher premium. That year, you don't die, so you pay another, higher premium. If you drop the coverage, not only do you lose the death benefit, but you also lose all the premium moneys that you paid in, and you lose the opportunity costs of those premiums. And that is eternal wealth through multiple generations lost forever. It's doing the opposite of many of the seven goals of wealth management: instead of reducing risk and increasing protection and having wealth to pass to the family, you're increasing risk, reducing protection, and leaving less wealth to your family.

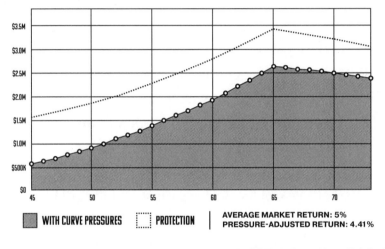

Fig. 6.2: Wealth Curve with term life halo effect.

Looking at an example where a 5 percent savings rate results in $2,642,000 accumulated over time, a twenty-year term life insurance policy creates a halo effect where more than one million dollars is above the assets. But that premium paid from the account reduces the wealth from $2,642,000 to $2,601,000.

That's a $41,000 opportunity cost on the premiums paid. And then, if the premium is not paid the next year, the policy's gone. It helped protect your wealth along the way, but how did losing the policy after all that time and all those premiums help to build your wealth?

Term insurance is an important part of every financial plan. But if all you're doing is holding it for the long term and then dropping it—like so many people do—that's not an efficient use of your money.

The life insurance that you own should actually add value to every stage of your financial plan. It should not take away from your wealth.

We recommend that clients have about 25 percent of their wealth in whole life insurance cash value with a permanent death benefit throughout the duration of their retirement plan. The key difference between term and whole life is that, in whole life, instead of the mortality cost at the end of the policy, it's amortized throughout the life of the policy.

There are many types of whole life insurance policies, but there are four fundamental principles with these:

1. **A guaranteed premium for a specific time frame.** For instance, a ten-pay policy is paid up in ten years. A twenty-pay policy is guaranteed to be paid up in twenty years. A whole life one hundred is guaranteed to be paid up at age one hundred. But no matter the term, the premium can never change; it's guaranteed to stay the same.

2. **A guaranteed cash value that the insurance company contractually returns to you in the future.** The guaranteed cash value builds as long as the premiums are paid. That means the cash value of a $1 million policy purchased by a forty-five-year-old would pretty much equal the death benefit at age one hundred.

3. **A guaranteed death benefit.** This means that your beneficiaries are guaranteed to receive a benefit. If you buy a $1 million policy and pay the premium, the death benefit is guaranteed all the way out to age 120.

4. **Dividends paid to the policyholder.** In the world of life insurance, there are mutual companies and stock companies. In a mutual company, you own a portion of the insurance company based on the policy that you have, and you share in the dividends of that contract. The dividend is your share of the profits of that insurance company.

Life insurance companies make money through investment portfolios—returns on bonds and mortgages and other investments. They also make money through what's called mortality science: the company insures people and expects that only a certain number of them will die in a certain period of time. For example, out of one thousand people insured in a year, only fifteen will die. If only ten die, then the company is profitable. Today, people are living longer, which is beneficial to life insurance companies because they are paying out claims later than expected. The mortality science part of the equation has nothing to do with the stock market or interest rates. It is based on risk. If an insurance company takes $20,000 from someone one day as premium for a $1 million policy, and the next day that person dies, then the company has to pay out—they've taken a bad risk and are now left to pay for that decision. That's why insurers require their insured to go through an extensive health exam before writing a policy. The healthier and less risk a person is based on that exam, the lower their premium.

Insurance companies also make money based on the lapse ratio. If you're paying a $645 premium for ten years and then get a bill for $10,200, you're probably going to drop the policy—you're going to let it lapse. At that point, the policy terminates, so the life insurance company is never obligated to pay the death benefit. Life insurance companies can count on that happening with term policies—the lapse ratio is predictable. They know it's going to happen every year like clockwork.

Finally, insurance companies make money by managing expenses. The better the insurance company manages its expenses, the better its portfolio, mortality science, and lapse ratio.

For example, a $1 million whole life policy with a premium of $19,608 started at age forty-six could have a guaranteed cash value of $452,610 twenty-four years into the contract at age seventy. The performance of the policy, along with reinvested dividends of $19,608, could accumulate $765,638—an extra $300,000-plus in dividend reinvestment. And the death benefit could be as much as $1,512,429.

The dividend in a whole life contract can be used for myriad options. You can use it to reduce your premium payment. You can let it accumulate in the policy (which is what is happening in the previous example). You can withdraw it and put it in something that draws interest. Or it can be paid to you in cash. If you reinvest it in the policy, it buys more insurance—as the money gets reinvested, the cash value grows at a greater rate than the guarantee, and the death benefit grows at a greater rate than the guarantee.

Dividends are not guaranteed. They never have been and never will be because they're based on the future. But once a dividend is paid and then reinvested back into a contract, it becomes part of your guarantees. That's how your guarantees actually get higher—once dividends are paid on the contract and reinvested, then they can never be taken away.

Here's what's really interesting. At age sixty-five with term life insurance, the death benefit is going to drop off. No more premiums, no more payout. Gone. But with a whole life policy, the halo effect is completely different.

If you were to take a portion of your money and reposition it to a whole life policy with an annual premium of $20,000, at age sixty-five, it would have a cash value of $575,000. Between your investment portfolio and cash, you would have $2,622,000. That's nearly the same amount of wealth as with no life insurance, but instead, you have a life insurance policy that has a 5 percent rate of return.

The questions you have to ask yourself are these: "Is my retirement going to be better off having just $2.6 million in the market? Would it be better to buy term and invest the difference, which basically gets me less money and more risk?" After all, that's what we've been taught—to buy term life insurance instead of whole life and then invest the difference. That's the way to make more money, right? But that's not really true. If you were to take 100 percent of the difference between a term life and whole life policy, and invest it in the S&P 500 during the 1989 to 2017 time frame with a 12 percent return, it might seem like your Wealth Curve would look like figure 6.3.

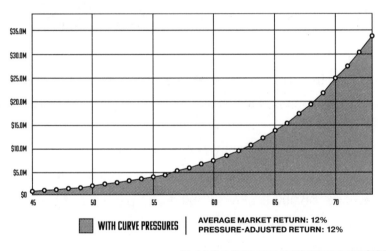

Fig. 6.3: Term life insurance and 12 percent return in S&P 500.

Why would you have money in a 5 percent whole life policy when you can get coverage with a term life and then get 12 percent in the market? At least that's what people often think will happen. They buy that life insurance that costs $1,000, and at age sixty-five, it will bring them $13,490,000.

Well, with everything in the S&P 500, you've got to factor in market volatility, rate of return, taxation based on gains, plus compound fees, giving you a Wealth Curve that looks more like figure 6.4.

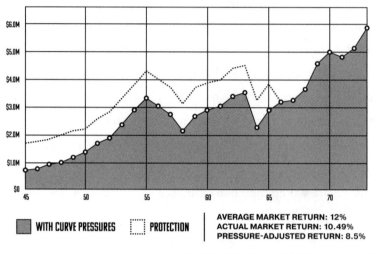

AVERAGE MARKET RETURN: 12%
ACTUAL MARKET RETURN: 10.49%
PRESSURE-ADJUSTED RETURN: 8.5%

Fig. 6.4: Term life with market volatility and compound taxes.

Compound taxes have taken the wealth from $13.4 million down to $5.9 million. Over twenty-nine years, taxes on the portfolio have amounted to $2.5 million.

And this doesn't even factor in fees. Even if fees are only 1 percent, over time, as the portfolio increases, that 1 percent will also grow—1 percent of $100,000 is only $1,000, but 1 percent of $1 million is $10,000. Market volatility, compound taxes, and compound fees can bring the account down to $2,892,000.

That's your wealth. The full story, not half the story. And it shows a world of difference from what people often think they're getting when they opt for a term life policy and stock market returns. If, for example, you actually had $14 million in returns at sixty-five when you retire, then the loss of a $1 million life insurance policy at that time might not be that impactful. But if you ended up with $2.8

million due to market volatility and compound taxes and fees, then $1 million in protection is a whole other story.

The argument that buying term and investing the difference will give you more money goes against the fundamental goals of reducing taxes, risk, fees, and costs, while increasing your savings rate and retirement income, putting more benefits and protection around your wealth, and ultimately, passing more to your family.

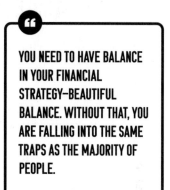

YOU NEED TO HAVE BALANCE IN YOUR FINANCIAL STRATEGY—BEAUTIFUL BALANCE. WITHOUT THAT, YOU ARE FALLING INTO THE SAME TRAPS AS THE MAJORITY OF PEOPLE.

I'm not saying it's bad to put your money in the S&P 500. I'm not saying don't invest your capital. What I'm saying is you need to have balance in your financial strategy—beautiful balance. Without that, you are falling into the same traps as the majority of people.

Compare the three scenarios of having whole life, term life, and no life insurance.

- With whole life, you could have $2,622,000 in total assets with $575,000 cash value and a death benefit of $811,000.

- With term life, you could have $2,601,000 in total assets, allowing you to have different investments, but you may ultimately lose your death benefit.

- With no insurance, you could have $2,642,000 in total assets, but no death benefit.

Which of these do you think would be better to have when entering retirement?

What we want is for you to keep your wealth. While buying the S&P 500 makes sense for part of a plan, it should not be an entire plan. Plus, we need to ensure that it's part of a strategy to pay less in taxes and less in fees and to have more benefits and more protection.

BENEFITS OF WHOLE LIFE

Think about all that you don't know right now about retirement. You don't know

- what inflation is going to be;

- what interest rates will be;

- what tax rates are going to be;

- how Social Security is going to be affected;

- how your pensions are going to be affected;

- how the market's going to perform; or

- how good your health is going to be.

And no one can tell you absolutes about these uncertainties either.

But there are a number of benefits with whole life policies that can actually help you in retirement and potentially even increase your income.

Waiver of premium. One of the benefits of a whole life policy is what's called a waiver of premium. If you were to become disabled at some point while the policy is in force, then the policy itself pays the premiums.

Increasing death benefit. A plus of the whole life policy, of course, is the death benefit, which pays your beneficiaries when you pass. Since there is guaranteed cash value on a whole life policy, it has value even if you pass prematurely.

Creditor proofing. In many states, the value of the policy is creditor proof, meaning it is not subject to the claims of creditors.

Dividends. A whole life policy has dividends, and those dividends have unique tax features. You can take those dividends in cash, or you can reinvest them back into the contract. If you have the dividend paid out to you in cash, you receive that tax-free until you reach your basis in the policy, which is premiums paid multiplied by the number of years you've paid premiums. That tax-free dividend does not appear on your tax return, which can be a huge benefit.

Loans. You can also take policy loans tax-free. When you borrow from your policy, you're actually borrowing from the premiums that you've paid in. You must pay back the loan, including interest, and failure to do so may make the loan taxable.

Since you might be able to get better interest rates elsewhere, then you can also use the death benefit of the policy as collateral for a loan from another source.

Volatility buffer. Portfolio withdrawals in a down market put pressure on the portfolio and increase the odds of running out of money exponentially. If you're in retirement mode and withdrawing in a down market, you could run out of money. (Remember my dad's saying? "Dying in a bad market is bad enough. But dying in a down market really sucks.") The life insurance cash value offers a volatility buffer. When the market is down, you could pull some income from your policy to use while the stock market portion of your portfolio returns.

Death benefit. When you die, the death benefit is passed to your heirs income tax-free (although state taxes may need to be paid).

Since the death benefit is guaranteed, it can also be used to increase the efficiency of your retirement plan as a tool to fight inflation. The death benefit, in essence, can replace all the assets that you spend in retirement. For instance, if inflation and taxes are high, and the only other place to get money is to accelerate the spend down of your other assets, then the policy can be annuitized to begin paying a certain amount of monthly income for a specific period of time.

Charitable remainder trust. With some policies, you can set up a charitable remainder trust, in which the policy is donated to a charity. The charity then invests the money from the policy and provides income from the investments back to the policyholder.

Accelerated death benefit. If you have what's known as an "accelerated death benefit," then you may be able to take a portion of the face value of the policy to help pay for expenses if you are terminal or chronically ill. In some policies, this benefit applies if you have long-term care expenses—so you get a dollar-for-dollar match from the policy for what you spend on long-term care.

As I write this book, my father is utilizing long-term care insurance, and my mother has a full-time job bickering with insurers to get proper reimbursement—my mother spends $4,000, she gets reimbursed for $3,000, and then she has to call up and fight for the other $1,000. When that is not part of a reimbursement strategy in a plan, then the whole life policy may pay for covered terminal or chronic illness.

Guaranteed cash value. The beauty of the cash value is that it is available at any time, and it is money that you can use to take advantage of opportunities.

Investing wisdom tells us that we have to buy in a down market—buy when there's blood in the streets, even if it's your own blood. So, for instance, when the market is down 30 percent, if your account has a value of, say, a couple of hundred thousand dollars, you could comfortably take a loan on that money and invest it in the stock market.

Those cash values are also accessible for multiple needs during the accumulation phase. But it must make economic sense to borrow against the policy.

When my wife and I had our third child, we needed a vehicle with a third row of seats. At the time, the popular car was a Dodge Durango, and the interest rates were about 7.5 percent to finance that car. But financing the car would mean getting a really good discount. So I bought the car and financed it, and then the next day took out a policy loan and paid off the 7.5 percent financing. I used the cash values, and then I paid my cash values back the same way I would've paid the credit company that lent me the money. That whole life policy allowed me to borrow $40,000, and the dividend was still getting credited to that contract the same way that it would've been if it were there. I paid a spread of about 0.5 percent—if the policy was making 6 percent, then I paid 6.5 percent. But I was paying myself instead of the company that was offering financing through the car dealership. Five years later, I had all my cash value back plus where the policy would have been, and we were having our fourth kid. Instead of borrowing from the policy at that time, I went with the zero-interest loans that were being offered at the time. I didn't need to use my policy then.

That's part of the beauty of a whole life policy. You can use the cash value strategically for opportunities or emergencies, and you're going to have more money with better tax treatment. In fact, my grandfather once told me that ready money was "Aladdin's lamp." By that he meant that liquid funds can open up tremendous opportunities when they present themselves, preventing you from racking up credit card debt and keeping you from selling assets at inopportune times.

Traditional financial planning says the only tool to fight inflation is the stock market. Well, because of volatility, that's not necessarily true. You can't predict whether the stock market will produce results when you need them.

With a whole life policy, the combination of the cash value and the death benefit makes for a tool at the foundation of your financial plan that is going to allow you to do multiple things in retirement that your neighbor can't do because they don't have it. It's all about the use of capital, yet it provides you with protection. With a strategy that has no insurance, you have to spend down your assets and try to preserve what you can to leave some for your family. With a whole life plan, you can spend the death benefit of the policy in creative ways and still have a death benefit to leave to your family. Otherwise, which retiree is having more enjoyment? The policyholder who has more money to spend in retirement or the one who has to work hard to preserve his money to leave to his family? The whole life policy lets you do both.

The key to a successful retirement plan is beautiful balance. With 20 to 30 percent of your net wealth in life insurance cash values with a death benefit, you will have substantial liquidation to cover taxes, healthcare costs, and other needs. Yet everybody jokes that the perfect retirement plan is to spend all your money and then die and leave your kids broke. How about we change the rules on that—let's make it so that you spend all your money and still give your kids all the money that you wanted to give them. Isn't that a better strategy?

While insurance for your car and home are typically something that we hope will never pay off, the truth is that death is going to occur at some point in time—somewhere between age zero and one-hundred-something. Are you going to be protected? Are you going to enjoy your money more fully during all those time frames? It's your choice.

REMEMBER:

- Life insurance is the only type of insurance with a definitive outcome.

- The goal is to have the maximum amount of coverage during your entire lifetime, owned in the most efficient manner.

- Paying for a life insurance policy and then letting it lapse when you retire defeats a wealth plan strategy.

- Life insurance protects your economic value.

- Buying term life and investing the difference in policy premiums in the stock market is taking a lot of risk.

- You need a beautiful balance in your wealth strategy.

- Benefits with whole life policies can actually help you in retirement and potentially even increase your income.

CHAPTER SEVEN

EDUCATION—THE KEY TO SMART WEALTH

One of the fundamental goals of a financial strategy is to maximize the wealth during your lifetime and pass on the maximum amount of wealth to your family. But most people generally perceive that having more money to pass on to family means sacrificing in one or more of the other six areas of a wealth plan: reducing taxes, reducing risk, reducing fees and costs, increasing savings rate, increasing retirement income, and putting more benefits and protection around your wealth.

There are a couple of other mindsets I see pretty consistently when it comes to leaving wealth to the next generation.

Some people don't want to leave anything to the kids; they plan to spend it all themselves or give it to a charity of choice. They may be self-made, and because they came into the world with nothing and had to work for everything, then their offspring should just do the same and fend for themselves.

Others want to leave all their wealth to the kids. They think that leaving the maximum amount of wealth to the kids in the future means giving up everything for themselves now. Often, I see parents in their seventies and eighties who never really made a lot of money, but who were very good at saving and built up a nice nest egg of maybe $2 million to $3 million over fifty years. Then they spend their retirement continuing to scrimp and save without enjoying all that they worked for. They end up leaving the bulk of their wealth to the next generation, and then that generation spends the money down in a couple of years.

> ❝
> IT ALL BOILS DOWN TO EDUCATION—TEACHING THE FAMILY AT AN EARLY AGE THE PRINCIPLES OF SAVING AND HARD WORK.

Building wealth for most people takes a lifetime. It's not easy because your wealth is constantly under attack. Taxes, fees, transaction costs, market volatility, bad decisions, overspending. What you do with your wealth in the bad times is more important than what you do with it in the good times.

It all boils down to education—teaching the family at an early age the principles of saving and hard work.

THE GENERATIONAL DISCONNECT

Strategically optimizing wealth comes down to communication between the generations. But when I talk to people, what I see missing are the core principles of wealth creation—understanding about growing wealth, enjoying it, and then passing it on. There seems to be a real disconnect between the generations when it comes to talking about wealth.

Most people starting out in their twenties or thirties don't make a lot of money, so they don't have a lot at their disposal and don't really understand what to do with what they have. Then there's the Great Depression–era people—they remember what it was like to be dirt poor, so hoarding money is the norm for them. They know how to save, but they don't know how to enjoy their wealth. Then there's the baby boomer generation who really didn't have a fear of loss—they had steady jobs and an abundance of food, sports, and recreation. Since then, there's a generation that has seen tremendous growth in incomes and lifestyles. Kids born into that lifestyle have become very accustomed to it. They've seen their parents' lives grow and improve—better cars, better vacations, goals achieved, and dreams coming true. People today have indulged their children to pursue great things, and they've been the benefactors of wealth. But when those kids try to leave the nest, they're shocked to find out just how much money it really takes to run a household.

This is where the generations need to teach those that follow them.

We have more opportunity in this country than pretty much any other country in the world. My generation just did what we had to do. We worked hard and too often placed the job ahead of family. Younger generations are bringing back balance; they are placing more importance on family and free time. As they enter the workforce, they are discovering the joy of work and the pain of failure—the feeling that comes from putting yourself out and not succeeding, but then learning from the experience and moving forward. There's a lot of talk about how the very young generation today will never be able to afford a house because of all their student loans. But I believe that as the younger generation comes into the workforce, they will start to understand what it means to work and earn a living. They'll begin to have goals—big goals—and they'll ultimately be a stronger generation than those that have gone before them.

Longevity has led to a quadruple stack of generations today—grandparents, parents, children, and grandchildren. So the need for multigenerational wealth education about saving and protecting wealth has never been more important.

PROTECTING AND PASSING WEALTH—UNDER ATTACK

Unfortunately, money is often a subject that families avoid, and as a result, people don't understand how to protect the wealth. The more open the conversation, the better future generations will be able to avoid pitfalls and traps that are placing that wealth under attack. It's your money, and you want to keep it. That goes for your parents' money too. If it's going to come to you, it must be managed properly so that it can be passed from one generation to the next.

Yet there is a fundamental misunderstanding of how to pass money well.

Currently, there are inheritance taxes at both the federal and the state levels, both of which are constant moving targets. States are changing them to adapt and keep residents from moving—that was a huge threat for a time. Retirees especially were moving to states that had low or no inheritance taxes. But the problem has begun to subside because of current federal exemptions at $11.4 million per person. If a husband and wife can pass on $22 million tax exempt, that may be the greatest gift ever given.

Historically, however, estate taxes have been known to devastate wealth. In 2012, there was a $5.4 million exemption that was expected to drop to $1 million. Fortunately, the $5.4 million was reaffirmed. But it's impossible to know what the trends will be in the future. If the rules change back, it could be devastating for many people—unless there's a good plan in place. That means people in their forties and fifties now need to be considering what will happen to their wealth when they are in their seventies or eighties. And when parents are in their seventies and eighties, that's when estates start showing up in the plans of forty- and fifty-year-olds.

If your parents die when you are in your fifties, then you are at a stage in life when you may have creditors. You may have some of the greatest creditors in your life. You may be a business owner who is suffering from a bad business economy, and all of a sudden, you inherit a lot of money directly in your name. Now that money becomes subject to your creditors. That's bad planning. You may have young children who are two to three years out from college and finances that are not in great shape, which would qualify your children for student loans. An inheritance at that point could reduce or eliminate that benefit.

And then there's divorce, with a fifty-fifty chance, based on current rates, that the marriage will end. If one spouse inherits money from a parent and that money is not comingled, then technically it is not part of a marital distribution where there's a trust that distributes X number of dollars mandatorily every single year. That's considered not to be an asset because it's an inherited asset. But in a divorce, the income that is generated from those assets is factored into the alimony or the palimony discussion. Let's say that you inherited $3 million and it's producing $90,000 a year in dividends and interest, money that you're not really touching but just letting grow. Then the marriage ends in divorce. That $90,000 is going to impact the divorce payouts.

Maybe you've accumulated a lot of your own personal wealth. If you inherit money on top of that, then you could end up in a higher tax bracket. The problem there is that may be taxed at the parents' level and then taxed again at your level. Depending on the state you live in, inheritance tax may put a significant drain on your wealth. You could be looking at 40 to 50 percent drains of wealth over multiple generations—in two generations, you could lose 75 percent of the wealth to taxes due to poor planning.

That's why the Wealth Curve Pressure Identifier conversation includes a discussion of the family. Are your parents still with us? Are they going to be an asset, or are they going to be a liability? Are you going to inherit money from them, or are they going to run out of money and end up needing your help? If the latter of these is the case, that might mean helping monetarily, or it might even mean taking time off work, which can be devastating to your wealth. But let's say you're going to inherit money from them. Do you want to take it into your name and have it exposed to all your potential creditors, or do you want to be strategic with it? That can mean setting up wills, trusts, revocable trusts, spousal lifetime access trusts, life insurance, limited liability corporations—all kinds of layers of asset protection become superimportant in the setup of multigenerational wealth.

Having all these things in place is going to really allow you to maximize the wealth and overcome so many of the potential threats.

SMART WEALTH—NOT ALL THAT EASY

When you look at some of the most successful families in our history, like the Rockefellers, the Kennedys, the Vanderbilts, and myriad others, you see some epic successes—and some epic fails.

The Rockefeller Foundation is one of the most successful foundations around. It was created with what's called a dynasty trust. A dynasty trust is an irrevocable trust that transfers wealth from generation to generation. The trust has allowed the family to protect the wealth from multigenerational attacks due to divorces, spendthrifts, inheritance tax, and other pressures. Multiple dynasty trusts along with some serious tax savviness protect the Kennedy fortune.

Then there are stories such as that of Cornelius Vanderbilt who, by anybody's measure, was one of the most successful people the world has ever seen. He accumulated a massive amount of wealth, but the family virtually has nothing today due to poor planning, poor protection, and poor tactics. That's not an uncommon story. The first generation makes a ton of money, the second generation begins draining it, and then by the third generation, the wealth is gone. It's estimated that the money doesn't last into the second generation for 70 percent of wealthy families, and it doesn't make it into the third generation for 90 percent.[12]

Preserving wealth generation to generation is about education and the protection pieces that are put in place, because we're all smart, but we all make some really stupid mistakes—that goes for even the wealthiest people.

An attraction known today as Castle in the Clouds is one example of that. The property was built in the early 1900s in the Ossipee Mountain Range in New Hampshire as an estate for a wealthy shoe manufacturer, Thomas Gustave Plant. After selling his business for millions, he retired to the mountains and acquired thousands of acres of land where he built his estate. Then, he lost a

---

12 David Kleinhandler, "Generational Wealth: Why do 70% of Families Lose Their Wealth in the 2nd Generation?" Nasdaq, October 19, 2018, accessed September 1, 2019, https://www.nasdaq.com/article/generational-wealth-why-do-70-of-families-lose-their-wealth-in-the-2nd-generation-cm1039671.

fortune to failed investments. Plant struggled to keep the estate but managed to stay in it until his death. The estate fell into disrepair and changed hands over time, until one owner recognized the value in one of its natural resources—water. For a time, the estate had a profitable bottled water operation, which eventually closed. Today, the property is owned by a conservation trust and is open to the public for tours. Its story is interesting in that a property that was created by wealth then saw a loss of that wealth, fell into decline, and then became a resource for recreating wealth.

> **EVEN THOUGH LESSONS ARE OFTEN LEARNED FROM THE MISTAKES PEOPLE MAKE IN THEIR WEALTH PLANS, THOSE CAN BE SOME OF THE COSTLIEST LESSONS EVER.**

Even though lessons are often learned from the mistakes people make in their wealth plans, those can be some of the costliest lessons ever.

You want your family to grow wealth. You want them to enjoy it. You want them to pass it on to another generation. But being smart with wealth is very difficult. It requires having open communication with family members, something that can be a very tough discussion.

The successful families whom I see in my practice are very open with each other about the wealth that they've created. Parents have engaged their children in the importance of hard work, spending within their means, and developing diversified strategies. At the same time, they are very prone to taking business risks. In their experience, that's where the money is really made.

Just look at my own family story. The Smallwood family originates from New Bern, North Carolina. Prior to the Great Depression, my family had cotton mills and lumberyards, and they were hardworking, successful entrepreneurs. My great-grandfather became a doctor because he was the best educated out of all of them, but with the onset of the Great Depression, people didn't have the money to pay for medical care, so they traded chickens and other goods for medical advice.

The Depression impacted the cotton mills and lumberyards to the point that they were eventually sold, and there was no money for my grandfather to go to college. So he borrowed some money, bought a boat, and fished for shad on the Neuse River, thinking that was the road to success. But the fish didn't run, and my grandfather ended up working in the engine room on a freighter to pay back his debts. That job brought him to New Jersey. He worked himself up to chief engineer, overseeing the engine room on major cruise lines and independents. Even though the wealth was gone by the time my grandfather wanted to go to college, he still made a good life for his family. His hard work gave my father a stable home and footing on which to pursue his dreams. My father and I, of course, both found success with our own firms, returning the family to its entrepreneurial roots.

IT TAKES A TEAM

In my firm, we have created an environment where the family, the wealth advisor, and the team of accountants, attorneys, and insurance agents comes together in a coordinated effort to work in the best interests of the client. We want to make it easier for families to have conversations about their wealth around the kitchen table to better ensure that wealth is protected and can be passed on in the most effective way.

Protecting wealth from all financial pressures should be the foundation of any wealth plan. It doesn't take a lot to put proper wills, trusts, and asset protections in place. But it does require consistency to stay up to date on new information, get clarity on changes that impact your plan, and work with a team of professionals who have the expertise to help you build your wealth. Nobody can do this by themselves.

We have also created the financial planning tools to develop a plan that lets you see where you are today and where you are headed. Then, we work together every year to see whether the decisions made last year are still working the way we want them to. We don't want you hanging on to decisions made ten years ago if they are no longer getting you where you want to be ten years from now.

The faster we learn what needs to change, make those changes, and keep improving the plan, the sooner you're going to reduce taxes, reduce risk, reduce fees and costs, increase your savings rate, increase your retirement income, put more benefits and protection around your wealth, and be able to pass your wealth on.

How do you open the conversation about wealth? The next chapter looks at the fundamental principles that should be part of that discussion.

REMEMBER:

- Passing the maximum amount of wealth on to family is one of the fundamental goals of a wealth plan.

- Education of family members is key to passing wealth down through the generations.

- Inheritance and estate taxes change over time, but planning can help protect a family's wealth.

- There are strategies for protecting wealth from divorces, spendthrifts, taxes, and other pressures.

- It takes a team—family, advisors, other professionals— working together to protect wealth for today and tomorrow.

THE FUNDAMENTAL PRINCIPLES

Now is the time to make changes. Ten years from now, you're going to be somewhere—is it where you want to be? The sooner you get your plan in line, the better off you will be when you retire.

The first step is to understand where your current plan is taking you. Do that before making any changes because if you don't understand your current plan, it doesn't matter where you are going.

Have your plan analyzed to see where it can be more efficient. Is it reducing taxes, reducing risk, reducing fees and costs, increasing savings rate, increasing retirement

> IT SHOULD NOT HAVE ALL YOUR EGGS IN ONE BASKET, BUT SHOULD INCLUDE BROAD, DIVERSIFIED STRATEGIES THAT HELP OFFSET TAXES AND INCLUDE PROTECTIONS. IT SHOULD HAVE WHAT I CALL "A BEAUTIFUL BALANCE."

income, putting more benefits and protection around your wealth, and passing more on to your family?

Whatever the components of your plan, the goal is to have it made easy, organized, and structured in the right way. It should not have all your eggs in one basket, but should include broad, diversified strategies that help offset taxes and include protections. It should have what I call "a beautiful balance."

Over the years, I've found that there are nine fundamental principles to a financial plan that can bring you that balance. Throughout the book, I've shared most of these with you. Let me recap those and share the rest of them with you here.

Principle 1: Maximize asset protection. The goal is to achieve maximum protection with the least amount of cost, and that protection should be secured up front so that you can continue to build savings and grow your wealth. There are five categories of protection:

- **Property and casualty coverage** to protect your home and car. This should include the proper amount of umbrella liability.

- **Disability insurance.** Your most valuable asset is your ability to work. If you were disabled yesterday, the odds of running out of money go up exponentially. If you are working and accumulating wealth, make sure you're protecting it.

- **Long-term care.** Maximizing protection from long-term care costs is not as simple as purchasing a policy. It's about understanding what your current income streams during retirement will be. It's about expenses and the position of your assets. And it's about how you release income and assets if an event occurs.

- **Wills and trusts.** It's important to get these in place to protect future generations.

- **Life insurance.** These are important not just during the accumulation phase, but also during retirement and the distribution phase.

Principle 2: Maintain a 15 percent or higher savings rate. This is one of the best ways to reach your wealth goals. If, for example, you make $100,000 annually, you should be saving $15,000 per year. As you make more money, your savings rate percentage should increase. As a reminder, here are our suggested savings rates:

- <$99,999.99: 10 percent
- <$199,999.99: 15 percent of $100,000
- <$499,999.99: 20 percent of $300,000
- <$999,999.99: 25 percent of $500,000
- >$1 million: 30 percent

Principle 3: Have 50 percent of annual expenses in liquid cash reserves. Remember what my grandfather used to say: "Ready money, available money, is like Aladdin's lamp." You need to have funds that you can access immediately, money that comes without surrender charges and is free of market volatility. Liquid funds open up tremendous opportunities, allowing you to take advantage of opportunities when they present themselves, preventing you from going into credit card debt (like when the refrigerator breaks), and keeping you from selling assets at inopportune times. The 50 percent rule is a vital step toward financial independence.

Principle 4: Have 25 percent of invested assets in whole life insurance cash value and a permanent death benefit for your entire life. This principle will help you have liquid assets while securing more income in retirement. One of the greatest fallacies about retirement is that you don't need life insurance, but the impact of a spouse passing can be devastating and mean a loss of income from pensions, Social Security, and health insurance benefits and subsidies. It can even move a survivor into another tax bracket, adding another layer of pressure to a wealth plan that now has half the resources and half the income.

Principle 5: Diversify your asset class investing. Spread out your money over different types of stocks. Invest in large cap, small cap, mid cap, value, growth, international, and emerging markets. Also, include different types of bonds and different types of alternative investments. Why? Because, historically, asset class performance changes—what's great today may not be so tomorrow. Along with that is the behavior of investors to sell low and buy high (instead of doing the opposite), and chasing returns can be a painful financial strategy.

Principle 6: Participate in company retirement plans up to the maximum match. Never pass up an employer match—since it's part of your compensation, make sure you're maximizing that benefit. That doesn't mean maxing out your 401(k) to the point of losing your liquidity. Although it's worth checking into qualified plans that offer pre- or post-tax payouts later, consider whether deferring taxes is actually going to be beneficial for you in the long run. Where will you be when it's time to take the money out? The answer is unique to you and your situation.

Principle 7: Maximize available tax deductions. The majority of people we meet do not maximize on the tax law. They are unaware of the deductions. As a result, they pay more taxes than they should. Taking advantage of deductions can help you be steps closer to financial independence.

Principle 8: Your primary residence should not exceed 25 percent of your gross annual income. If you make $100,000 and the payment principal, interest, and taxes for your primary residence exceed $25,000 a year, odds are you won't save any money. Too much of your money is going to that house. And there are other expenses that come with it as well. In retirement, your primary home should not exceed 25 percent of your gross net worth. A $2.5 million house, for example, is not going to be sustainable in retirement if your net worth is $5 million because the expenses to maintain such a home are too high and its appreciation will likely be too low. The proportion of your plan should be 75 percent income-generating assets and 25 percent of what I call income-sucking assets.

Principle 9: Have a goal of Social Security, pension, and guaranteed income sources covering more than 60 percent of your annual expenses in retirement. By the time you hit retirement, ideally have very predictable, strong, conservative income sources that are not subject to volatility or variability ready to provide you with the majority of your annual income in retirement. Optimizing these principles is the best way to have a healthy, balanced financial plan that keeps you on the path to financial independence.

HIRING A FINANCIAL ADVISOR

Hiring a financial advisor is an important decision, and there are thousands of advisors that you can choose. Before hiring someone to help you with your wealth planning, ask questions to better understand their practices and whether they are in line with your needs. Here are some essential questions to get you started.

1. **What scope of work do you provide advice on?** A full spectrum of advice is the key to success, and every recommendation should be unique to you.

2. **What is your experience, education, and licensing?** It is important that an advisor have a CFP®, Series 7, 63, and Life Insurance License. Also ask about experience—how long have they been providing advice? Have they seen or studied the trends to understand that everything in a plan can change from one year to the next?

3. **Do your financial calculations account for the impact of taxation?** Most financial software ignores the impact of taxation on your assets, creating a false sense of wealth creation. An advisor should understand that taxation is a part of wealth planning.

4. **Do your financial calculations use average rates of return or market volatility adjusted returns?** Investors do not receive average returns; they earn returns that are impacted by market volatility. That creates two different outcomes.

5. **Do you deploy a single-focus investment strategy and make all portfolio choices?** Is the advisor focused on selling a single product? Or do they view products as tools to create a comprehensive plan for you? Passive, active, tactical, and alternative investments all play important roles in the best plans.

6. **Do you have a support team and implementation network?** Most advisors share a support person, and everything is dependent on the advisor doing everything. Look for a team.

7. **Do your recommendations incorporate asset protection ideas unique to my circumstances?** Your unique set of financial variables requires a design customized to you, not to your neighbor.

Too many advisors connect themselves to a product, and that product becomes the solution to all of your problems. That is fundamentally wrong. Your advisor must be macro minded. They must bring multiple disciplines to the table to be able to source the things that are most important to you. They don't need to be an expert, but they need to be able to know how to source, find, and sift through solutions and make good decisions with you.

My mentor, Robert Castiglione, talked about the macro advisor and would say, "When was the last time you sat with all of your advisors in the same room at the same time and built a plan for you?" The answer to that question by most people is "Never."

You need a macro advisor at the helm so you can focus on earning your wealth. As Strategic Coach® Dan Sullivan says, it's about doing things differently; that's how you work smarter, not harder. Surround yourself with great teams, and you'll be able to do more of what you love and less of what you don't love doing. That's how you gain financial freedom, enjoy your wealth, protect it, and then pass it on to future generations.

NOW IS THE TIME

Financial success—financial freedom—is not one thing. It's a combination of everything you do, every single day. It comes from the way you address your money, think about money, and respect your money. The goal is to have a plan that allows you to enjoy your money today and to have financial freedom tomorrow.

Over time, the advice that we've given, and the advice that we continue to provide, has evolved as we've become more seasoned in what we're doing. At my firm and in my personal life, a lot has changed since I started in this business—good and bad. I've been through several business partners for various reasons, family illnesses, and the bursting of the dot-com and real estate bubbles.

Through it all, we've developed financial tools that support us as we advise clients that the way to achieve financial freedom is to make a plan and then revise that plan over and over again. That plan should be focused on reducing taxes, reducing risk, reducing fees and costs, increasing savings rate, increasing retirement income, putting more benefits and protection around your wealth, and having wealth to pass on to family.

You've got to have a plan. Without a plan, you're going to end up somewhere, but probably not where you want to be. Now is the time to get your plan in line. The sooner you get started, the better off you will be when it comes time to retire.

When you make that plan, know that it will need corrections. Things will likely get out of balance, but that's part of life. Just make some changes, and keep moving toward your goal. Think of those goals like the horizon—always in the distance, always something to move toward. Like being in a boat on the ocean and rowing toward a horizon that is always there, awaiting your arrival.

When working toward those goals, remember that financial freedom is not simply being able to retire from the daily grind. It's about being able to do exactly what you want to do, when you want to do it, with whomever you want. It's about continuing to grow your life, a mentality of abundance, not scarcity. It's not about hoarding your wealth and everything you have; it's about continuing to look for opportunities, for ways to improve, for better outcomes. That's financial freedom—it's being able to walk away from things you don't like or want to do, and doing only those things you love. One of my earliest clients, who is still with me, has the concept of a walkaway fund. It's an amount of money sitting in the bank that has grown over the years, and it allows her to walk away from any situation at any time. That's powerful; that's real financial freedom.

Financial freedom is being in control of your wealth and having a realistic understanding of what your wealth can do—and what it can't do. It's about growing your wealth, income, free time, contribution to your market, contribution to society as a whole. And it's about you—growing as a person.

Motivational speaker Jim Rohn compares wealth to the four seasons. In spring, he says, you sow the seeds. In summer, you nurture the seeds. In fall, you reap the harvest. Then winter sets in—personal winters, market winters, political winters, tax winters. Financial freedom is knowing how you're going to weather those winters, short or long.

The markets are going to ebb and flow. Your income is going to ebb and flow. It doesn't mean your plan is broken. With the right reserves, you can be buffered from the ebb and flow and continue to move toward your horizon.

Financial success, financial freedom, doesn't come from buying one thing or doing one thing. It's the accumulative financial decisions that are made every single day. If you set goals for savings, protections, lifestyle, business, and you hit all those goals, if you make well-thought-out changes to your plan, you're going to

I WANT YOU TO ENJOY YOURSELF NOW.

get to your number. But don't put pressure on yourself to retire at a certain age just because life is short and you've got to stop at some point and start enjoying yourself.

I want you to enjoy yourself now.

Proper planning with the proper team will put you in a better position. You'll experience reduced taxes, reduced risk, and reduced fees and costs. You'll increase your savings rate and retirement income. You'll have more benefits and protection around your wealth. And you'll pass more to your family. If you want all those things for today and tomorrow, then we absolutely want to work with you.

APPENDIX

HISTORY OF INCOME TAX RATES ADJUSTED FOR INFLATION

YEAR	# OF BRACKETS	FIRST BRACKET RATE [%]	TOP BRACKET RATE [%]	TOP BRACKET INCOME	TOP BRACKET ADJUSTED 2014	COMMENT
1913	7	1	7	$500,000	$11.86M	FIRST PERM. INCOME TAX
1917	21	2	67	$2.0M	$11.86M	WORLD WAR I
1925	23	1.5	25	$100,000	$1.34M	POSTWAR REDUCTION
1932	55	4	63	$1.0M	$17.14M	DEPRESSION ERA
1936	31	4	79	$5.0M	$84.45M	--
1941	32	10	81	$5.0M	$79.86M	WORLD WAR II
1942	24	19	88	$200,000	$2.75M	REVENUE ACT 1942
1944	24	23	94	$200,000	$2.88M	INDIVIDUAL INCOME TAX ACT OF 1944

YEAR	# OF BRACKETS	FIRST BRACKET RATE (%)	TOP BRACKET RATE (%)	TOP BRACKET INCOME	TOP BRACKET ADJUSTED 2014	COMMENT
1946	24	20	91	$200,000	$2.41M	--
1964	26	16	77	$400,000	$3.03M	VIETNAM WAR REDUCTIONS
1965	25	14	70	$200,000	$1.49M	--
1981	16	14	70	$215,400	$563,000	REAGAN ERA CUTS
1982	14	12	50	$85,600	$211,000	REAGAN ERA CUTS
1987	5	11	38.5	$90,000	$186,000	REAGAN ERA CUTS
1988	2	15	28	$29,750	$59,000	REAGAN ERA CUTS
1991	3	15	31	$82,150	$142,000	OMNIBUS BUDGET RECONCILIATION ACT OF 1990
1993	5	15	39.6	$250,000	$406,000	OMNIBUS BUDGET RECONCILIATION ACT OF 1993
2003	6	10	35	$311,950	$398,000	BUSH TAX CUTS
2011	6	10	35	$379,150	$396,000	--
2013	7	10	39.6	$400,000	$403,000	AMERICAN TAXPAYER RELIEF ACT OF 2012

ABOUT THE AUTHOR

John L. Smallwood is a Certified Financial Planner and president of Smallwood Wealth Management, which provides investment consulting and financial plan design for corporate executives, entrepreneurs, and professionals. John's strength lies in his commitment to continually improving and quality of the planning process. He aims to provide a process for repositioning assets to help decrease risk, decrease taxation, and increase protection. He is the creator of the Wealth Curve and author of *5 Ways Your Wealth Is Under Attack*.

John graduated from Bentley College with a BS in economics and finance and has given conference talks and lectures at the University of California, Berkeley's Haas School of Business; the University of North Carolina at Chapel Hill's Kenan-Flagler Business School; and Johns Hopkins, among others. He was named a Five Star Wealth Manager every year from 2011 to 2016 by Five Star Professional.

John and his wife, Sharon, reside in Shrewsbury, New Jersey, with their children, Jack, Jared, Christopher, and Eve. Jack graduated from the University of Pennsylvania in 2018, Jared attends the Gabelli School of Business at Fordham University, Chris attends the Whitman School of Management at Syracuse University, and Eve is in high school.

ACKNOWLEDGMENTS

Without my client relationships and all the wonderful deep conversations over the years, these concepts could not have been developed—thank you. Without John P. Smallwood, my father/business partner/mentor, I surely would have been a casualty of the industry. Above all my wife, Sharon, has provided me with the confidence, clarity, and strength to make my dreams into reality. Together we have four amazing children, Jack, Jared, Christopher, and Eve, who have given me the desire and reason to be part of their lives.

I would like to thank Leanne Menzel, my right hand in helping me coordinate my life to make time to create this, and the team at Advantage Media for helping organize my thoughts and message.

OUR SERVICES

Our clients choose Smallwood Wealth because they have reached a level of financial success that they know they need assistance in managing. They want a big picture approach to wealth management, looking at all the aspects of their plan.

OUR JOB

Current financial circumstances are unique to each individual. Our collaborative approach organizes your financial assets and strategy to help you make sense of what you own and, more importantly, understand how financial pressure can impact your wealth and its potential.

THE GOAL

Our goal is to help you develop financial strategies that attempt to reduce risk and taxes, accumulate more wealth, enhance retirement income, and pass more assets on to your family. Our focus is completely on you and your financial goals.

THE WEALTH CURVE PROCESS OVERVIEW

The Smallwood Wealth Investment Management Process follows five main steps. The first step, the Wealth Curve Conversation, is a holistic approach and an in-depth discovery of your lifestyle, your financial situation, your risks, and your goals. We aggregate all the aspects of your current financial plan into one big picture, called the Wealth Curve Blueprint. This will show you the opportunities and deficiencies of your current plan. We then move on to step three, the Wealth Curve Scorecard. This scorecard is a powerful visual tool that highlights where your plan is strong and where it needs some attention. In step four, we will run the Wealth Curve Simulation. Here we analyze your plan to show under which real-life scenarios your plan will perform strongly or weakly. In essence, this is a stress test of your plan. The final step is the Wealth Curve Implementation. After carefully analyzing, simulating, and creating adjustments to your plan, it is now time to put it into action.

facebook.com/SmallwoodWealthManagement/

linkedin.com/in/john-l-smallwood

twitter.com/smallwoodwealth